# The Gospel of the Beloved Disciple

# The
# GOSPEL
## *of the*
# BELOVED
# DISCIPLE

James P. Carse

HarperSanFrancisco
*A Division of HarperCollinsPublishers*

HarperCollins Web Site: http://www.harpercollins.com

HarperCollins®, 🅐 ®, and HarperSanFrancisco™ are trademarks of Harper-Collins Publishers Inc.

FIRST EDITION

Designed by Laura Lindgren

Library of Congress Cataloging-in-Publication Data
Carse, James P.
    The gospel of the beloved disciple / James P. Carse.—1st ed.
      p.   cm.
    ISBN 0-06-061576-1 (cloth)
    ISBN 0-06-061577-X (pbk.)
    1. Bible. N.T.—History of Biblical events—Fiction.   2. Women in the Bible—Fiction.   3. Jesus Christ—Fiction.   I. Title.
    PS3553.A7664G67    1997
    813'.54—dc21
                                                          97-17856

97 98 99 00 01 RRD 10 9 8 7 6 5 4 3 2 1

*For Donna*

# TO THE READER

The gospel is a literary form unique to Christianity. The first gospel to be composed is probably that attributed to Mark, written some thirty years after the death of Jesus. By the end of the second Christian century scores of gospels had been written.

Each gospel was written to declare the truth of Jesus' life and teaching. However, because the evangelists relied partly on a collective memory and partly on their own imaginations, there are as many interpretations of the life of Jesus as there are gospels.

In the year 325, Constantine, emperor of Rome, called a conference in the small Anatolian city of Nicea to settle the doctrinal disputes dividing Christendom and threatening the stability of the empire. At this conference, four gospels—Matthew, Mark, Luke, and John—were designated canonical. All others were excluded.

Since that time the writing of gospels has largely died out. In fact, of the excluded gospels, only fragments of about thirty-five are extant. Only one, the Gospel of Thomas, has survived in its entirety.

Nicea gave Christendom a canon but it did not solve a number of persistent questions about the gospels. Not only scholars, but ordinary readers, have long noted the discrepancies. The birth stories of Luke and Matthew, for example, have almost nothing in common with each other. The Jesus of John could not have recognized himself in the Jesus of Mark, still less in the Jesus of Thomas.

This is not to say that these many gospels were merely whimsical creations. Each is written out of a concrete historical moment and thus reflects the distinctive conviction and passion of its author. The complete gospels as we have them see Jesus with Christian eyes colored by more than half a century of experience, mostly confusing and often painful. How to relate to the pagan world around them, how to resolve the dissension among themselves, and, later, how to respond to Roman persecution—all these issues shaped their memory of the past and their hopes for the future.

There has long been a desire among scholars to get closer to the historical Jesus by filtering out the "christianizing" elements that would have seemed puzzling to Jesus and his immediate followers. The task is not easy. At best, there is only a rough consensus on what Jesus was not: he was not primarily a miracle worker, nor a self-denying ascetic, nor a political activist. It is most unlikely that he thought of himself as the messiah. He does seem to have been a sort of wandering sage and countercultural visionary who taught by story and brief trenchant observation.

The most secure historical fact is that Jesus was executed. All of the gospels, canonical and noncanonical, seem agreed on this; and it is confirmed by independent writings contemporary to the New Testament. But when we ask what crime he was executed for and whether he was executed by the Jews or the Romans, the gospel accounts are inconclusive.

Therefore, when the image of Jesus has been cleansed of its later Christian emendations, only ghostly echoes remain, certainly not the striking figure he must have been to his contemporaries.

This leaves us with an insistent question: Is it possible to draw a historically credible picture of Jesus as the first-century Jew he most certainly was? Are we warranted, in sum, in resuming the early Christian practice of writing gospels as a way of presenting the mystery and the meaning of the life of Jesus?

We must of course abandon the claim that we can reach back to the "real" Jesus. That was never possible, even for the earliest evangelists. We must do as they did: let the unique and terrible experience of our own century reflect itself in our writing about another. While hard facts about the life of Jesus himself are scarce and controversial, a great deal is known about Herodian Palestine, even the region of Galilee where he spent most or all of his life. There is also a large body of Jewish literature dating roughly from the time of Jesus that can serve as a guide to the social and religious issues that confronted him and as a model for the way he would have addressed them. Jesus was no doubt a storyteller. This literature is rich with the kinds of stories he likely told.

These sources do not write a gospel by themselves. What is needed, now as before, is imagination, but an imagination that takes no more liberty with the known historical material than the earlier gospels themselves took. Luke and John and Thomas cannot all be right, neither are they all wrong. Each wrote a gospel grounded in the time of Jesus and their own time. Why should we do less?

It was as they had heard. The Samaritan was living at the edge of the Lake of Galilee in an abandoned fisherman's shack. When they came upon her, she was staring out at the horizon and only slowly seemed to recognize them.

Too old now to tend a garden or even to net minnows from the shallow edge of the sea, she lived on the scraps left by the fishermen after they had cleaned their catches and on the crusts of bread they sometimes shared with her.

Hunger had pulled her skin tight in a way that disguised her age. But the years showed in her eyes. They focused slowly and had little light in them.

Seeing how time had lain its burden on her, they hesitated.

Joram, the scribe, was the first to speak.

"There have been many rumors. Some believe you were sold into slavery by the Romans, or secretly executed. Others have said that you were taken up with Jesus into paradise."

The old woman shook her head and smiled faintly.

"It is not only you who are the subject of rumor," Joram continued. "Many strange stories are being told about Jesus, especially the last year of his life, the year you knew him."

"And about what happened afterward," said another of the visitors.

"We sometimes meet wanderers who report amazing visions or prophesy the events to come at the end of time. Not a year ago, returning from a meal with some of the others in Emmaus . . . "

"It is you, Havah," the old woman said.

"Yes, it's Havah."

"I did not know you at first. You were but a child, and now . . . "

"We have suffered much," Havah said. "We have also heard and seen much. The stranger I met coming from Emmaus asked me if I knew how the great temple in Jerusalem was destroyed. 'Yes,' I said. 'The Romans did it. Who doesn't know that?' 'It was not the Romans,' he told me, 'for I saw with my own eyes an invisible arm reach up from the earth and strike it repeatedly with a stake, the very stake the Romans use to . . .'" She looked down at her hands.

"And a stranger once told me," said another of the visitors, "he was looking for the tomb of a certain great rabbi. 'How can I help you find it if I don't know the name of this rabbi,' I said to the stranger. He said, 'This tomb is empty; you will know who this rabbi is if you know why the tomb is empty.' 'I don't understand,' I told him. He walked away, saying nothing more."

"Many of us," said another, leaning toward the old woman and speaking softly, "have come to believe that these strangers may be Jesus himself, that he did not die after all."

Another spoke. "Do you recognize me? I am Didymos."

"Yes, I recognize you, Didymos."

Didymos moved closer. "I tell you I was visited by him one night. He stood above my bed. He said, 'Touch my wounds.' I looked and saw that his wounds were still fresh. Then he spoke again. 'I cannot die until you touch me.' I sat up and said, 'You live then?' 'Touch me,' he said in a stern voice. I did as he said. He vanished at once. What am I to make of this?"

A strong wind had risen and was coming off the lake. Threads of gray hair blew across the old woman's face. Her eyes followed the seagulls floating on the wind. Then she turned to Didymos.

"His death released you."

For a moment no one spoke.

"We did not come to share these rumors with you," said the scribe, Joram. "We came because too many claim the authority to speak for him." He unrolled a thick scroll. "The time has come when we must make a careful record of what happened, a gospel, a history of what he did and said among us. How else will those who never knew him understand?"

"What happened to the girl—Martha?" she asked.

No one spoke for a moment.

"She was seen on the streets of Ganim," Havah answered. "Her life has been hard. She would not speak of our time together. 'I wish only this,' she said, 'that I had never heard his name nor seen his face.' Then she walked away."

"And Bartholomew?"

"Nothing. Nothing at all."

"Yaakov?"

"The hills north of Zoar."

Joram held the scroll where she could see its words. "We have read this to all the living we could find. There were many corrections. Your memory is the most precious of them all. You knew him before the rest of us. He talked with you as with no other."

She ran her finger across the parchment. "I can barely read this. My eyes . . . "

"Antonius will read it to you."

The Roman, marked with scars of warfare or of prison, stood next to Joram and read the words with a scholar's precision.

After a while he paused, midway through a sentence. "We speak of you here. We call you . . . the beloved disciple."

She said nothing.

"In the months we were together," Joram said, "we knew you only as the Samaritan woman, the one Jesus loved."

Antonius resumed his reading. She was so still it was not certain she heard any of it. Then, suddenly, she placed her frail hand against the manuscript. "Read that part again."

The Roman read the passage once more and waited for a response, but she only nodded at him to continue. She asked for several more repetitions but still without comment.

As Antonius was reading words spoken by Jesus to a crowd, she said, "No, it wasn't exactly like that."

Joram leaned forward, prepared to alter the text.

"He spoke those words, yes," she said to Joram. "But something else happened in that place. The silence of the people when he spoke. I remember a woman's sigh. That sigh is stronger than the words you have written here."

"This can be added to the scroll," Joram said. His fingers circled above the manuscript as he searched for a phrase and for a place to insert it into the text. But he wrote nothing. Instead he signaled the Roman to continue reading.

The beloved disciple stopped him soon again.

"The last time we ate together, on our way up to the city. I hear nothing of that."

"But he did not eat with us. He divided the bread and poured the wine but touched none of it himself. Why, I don't know."

"We feasted on his hunger," she said. "We were drunk with his thirst."

Joram stared at her but said nothing. Antonius resumed his reading. Some of the others suggested changes. Joram wrote brief notes between the lines of his scroll or wet his thumb to rub out a word and replace it with another. Sometimes he added a longer sentence along the margin, careful to hold down his treasured document against the occasional violence of the wind.

So absorbed were they in this discourse, no one but Joram noticed that the sun had dropped below the mountains.

"Somewhere there is an end to this," he said, rapping on the much amended text.

The old woman had turned away. She was now little more than a profile, standing against the last light in the sky. The wind was stronger. The thin cloth of her hooded robe slapped against her face.

"If I can't write a final word," Joram protested, "there can't be a gospel."

The old woman took hold of the scroll; it fell open. "There is too much to say to end it here," she said to the scribe.

"But then there will be no conclusion to our writing and speaking with each other about these events," Joram replied. "There will always be more to say."

"That more," she said, "that is the gospel."

She lifted the scroll to the wind. It swept upward as though it had wings of its own then spiraled slowly out over the water. Because of the darkness, it was impossible to see where the water received it.

Stunned, they did not notice at first that she was walking away from them along the edge of the sea.

"Where are you going?" Havah called.

She turned back briefly, but said nothing more.

The birds gathered behind her, pecking at her footprints. No one moved or spoke. Soon they could see only the birds, then only the dark.

# The Gospel of the Beloved Disciple

# I

As soon as there was light they went into the fields to pre-pare them.

Bent over their wooden mattocks, they turned up the soil in long, even furrows. Small birds followed, pecking at the fresh earth.

When the sun was full upon them, one of the girls stood and looked at a boy working near her.

"Did you say something to me?"

He, too, stood.

"No," he said.

"But I heard someone speak."

The boy hesitated for a moment. "What did you hear?"

She looked down. An earthworm was coiling back into the broken earth.

She turned to the boy and felt something she had never felt before, then resumed her work so he would not see what was happening.

When it started to get dark, she looked over her shoulder and found he was staring at her.

"Miryam?"

He said nothing more but she understood. She did not answer at once because she was afraid.

"Yes."

She could feel the uncultivated soil pressing against her foot.

# 2

After the rains came and the seeds began to sprout, the boy made a small house with mud and straw, framing it with strong green branches cut from acacia trees. It was his first roof but the ground under it remained dry.

They were the same age but she seemed younger. When spoken to she often looked up but said nothing, as though she were in a dream. Sometimes she would sit in one place, curled on her feet, her eyes bright and unfocused, staring at nothing. Some thought she was backward, others that she had a secret knowledge.

The boy thought nothing, but occasionally her oddness made him treat her roughly.

It was mostly at night that she heard the voice. The first time she heard it she woke the boy. He asked her what the voice said and when she could not find the words to repeat what she had heard, he quickly became angry. The next time he struck her and warned her never to wake him again.

One night she heard someone call her name. "Miryam." At first she thought it was the boy. She sat up and saw that he was still asleep. "Miryam," she heard again.

This time it was not one voice but many. She was afraid and pressed her hands against her ears. The voices continued. Now, it was not because he had threatened her that she did not wake Yosef, but because for once she understood what the voices said.

She lay back, unable to sleep. It was spring. Everywhere the earth was in flower. So the child would come in the winter.

# 3

The soldier woke just before dawn. It was not the captain who woke him but a dream. In the dream he saw the faces of the children and their mothers. They were all laughing at him, all but one. This one sat by herself and looked away. The laughter mocked him and his sword. There was blood on the sword and when he touched it he saw that it was not the blood of the children. It was the sword itself that was bleeding. Then the one who sat alone turned toward him.

"So then it's you," she said.

There was no mockery in her. Though she was a girl herself, she spoke with the voice of a mother. He knew the voice. It was that of the mother who died at his own birth. Then the girl held up her son. She was offering the child to him as a gift when he woke.

He felt the tightening across his chest. He buried his face lest the other soldiers should wake to see what showed in it.

The dream was far worse than what he had to do. He was a soldier and he did what soldiers do. He killed the children because he was commanded to do it. Sometimes he even laughed with the others.

After a breakfast of uncooked barley soaked in sweet wine, he forgot the dream and began the day's labors. Before the high heat of midday they had gone through three more villages. Then they came to a collection of ragged houses too few to be called a village. The mothers and their children were in hiding.

The captain brought a youth to be questioned. Though the youth was more boy than man, he was old enough to have a child of his own.

"There are no women and no children here," he told the soldier.

The soldier struck the boy's hand with the flat side of his sword, then ordered him to show where his own child was hidden. Begging not to be hit again, the boy led him up the hill and stopped before a disordered pile of straw and withered palm branches.

The soldier kicked all this away and exposed the huddled body he knew would be there. The way she was coiled around the baby, he could not kill the child without killing both of them. He pulled her back. When she looked up at him, he recognized her face. It was the one in the dream, the one who did not laugh at him.

The girl did not move, just looked back at the soldier unblinking. He held the sword at his side, the other hand resting on a flaying knife thrust in his belt.

The child reached toward a small moth trying to free itself from the remains of a spider web.

# 4

It had been at daybreak, that very morning, that someone came up from a village by the sea to say that the soldiers were coming that day and to hide at once. The rumor then was true. They were killing the male children and attacking some of the mothers.

Miryam strapped the child to her breast and walked with Yosef up the long hill to the field where they had harvested their first crop.

She tucked herself into a depression in one of the large basalt rocks rolled off to the edge of the field. The boy gathered enough palm branches and straw to cover them.

When Miryam later heard Yosef's pleading as he came up with the soldier, she knew that he had been tortured. Since there was no way she could protect the child, she curled around him so they would die together.

The soldier tore back the cover and stood silently for a moment.

When he touched her shoulder, it was not as she had expected. He lifted her back gently so he could see the child. She looked up at him. He held a sword at his side, his other hand rested on a flaying knife stuck in his belt. He stared into her face for a moment but said nothing.

Then he lifted his sword. Holding it in both hands, he raised it above them. It made a terrible noise when it hit the rock. The next time, the blade cut through the palm branches, throwing some of them back over the mother and child. The soldier, careful not to hit them, continued to swing with a throaty roar as though he were slaughtering the whole village at once.

When he finally stopped, Miryam and the baby were covered with a thick mat of straw and palm leaves. The soldier was sucking in great breaths. For a moment she thought his breathing sounded like a child trying not to cry.

"Hallo!" someone called from below. "You found them?"

"I found them," he gasped.

Through the palm leaves Miryam saw the soldier kick Yosef

to the ground then lift and kick him again, driving him down the hill. To the other soldiers, he described in large gestures how he had done away with the mother and child.

# 5

"Do not move from this place," his father told him. He put a small pile of odd wooden pieces before the boy and went back to his work. Jesus tried to make a house of the pieces like his father was doing but they quickly fell apart.

The child walked to the edge of the meadow and watched the insects flashing in the sun. He held out his hand and stood quiet as a tree. A small dark butterfly with yellow eyes on its wings rested lightly on his fingers. He blew on it until it swam off in the wind.

He lifted the corners of his cloak, like wings, and danced into the meadow.

His father found him hours later. He wasn't lost, he told his father. He was following the little bird.

# 6

Sitting on the threshing floor with the other children, Jesus was tying chaff into tight bundles.

Someone called his name in a loud whisper. His cousin Yohanan was standing in the doorway. Jesus stepped softly toward him. Certain no one was watching, they ran down the hill toward the river.

When they came to the place where the river eddied, making a large shallow pool, they separated, Yohanan walking the high rim of the bank, Jesus hunting in the dense stand of marsh grass at the water's edge.

Several frogs and a salamander angled off, too quick for his bare hands. He found a heavy stick and stuck it through his belt like a sword.

Peering into the deeper grass, he saw a turtle, not three arm lengths away, sunning itself on a rock, head up and alert. He stalked it, holding his breath, mimicking the stealth of the egrets.

The turtle started but Jesus was quick enough to stun it with his sword before it hit the water.

He turned it upside down on the rock and waited. When nothing happened, he gave the turtle a solid blow. Still nothing happened. He turned it over, hit it again, then again, harder. Its shell shattered.

He looked up. Yohanan was gaping at him with a wild and unblinking stare.

Jesus kicked the remains of the turtle into the river where it turned slowly in the current, trailing threads of gore. He turned back to his cousin.

Yohanan had found a honeycomb and was carrying it on his head as the wandering ascetics do, his face streaked with thick yellow lines.

# 7

In his twelfth year Miryam prepared Jesus to make the long walk up to Jerusalem where he would read from the sacred texts in the temple.

As they made their way along the crowded road at the approach to the city, they came upon soldiers dragging and prodding a crowd of ragged children.

"Where are they taking these children?" Miryam asked a stranger.

He nodded in the direction of a scarred hill above the city. A forest of huge crosses had been planted atop it. On some of them they could see the twisted profiles of the dead and dying. Large dark birds spiraled above.

"Why?" Jesus asked.

The stranger shrugged. "The soldiers are cleaning the streets of whores and thieves."

One of the girls suddenly broke from the group and ran with her arms out toward Miryam. When a soldier came after her, the girl threw a stone that struck him on the cheek. In his rage he held her down and drew his flaying knife.

Miryam pulled Jesus away. A few steps later he turned back and saw what the soldier was doing.

# 8

The next morning, when the guards had pushed open the massive doors of the temple, they entered with a crowd of worshipers, merchants, beggars, and cripples. Paralytics were carried on makeshift pallets or on the backs of friends. Animals for sacrifice were led to their cages. A small crowd of lepers was locked into a barred enclosure in one corner of the vast space.

Here and there were other twelve-year-olds who had come with their parents for the ceremonial reading of the texts.

Dressed in the rude, one-piece tunic of the country, Jesus drew looks from the city youths.

When his turn came to approach one of the great scrolls, he stepped up and placed his hands on it. With an unchanging expression on his face, he began to speak without looking at the written word, exactly as the illiterates do.

"I am no prophet, nor a prophet's son," he began, "but a voice asked me, 'What did you see?' I see that you plant the wicked and the wicked take root. The ax knows its master, but the people of Israel does not know its God."

Several priests and Levites passing through the crowd of

11

waiting youths stopped and turned toward the boy as he continued in a quiet voice. A scribe was with them.

"He says, 'Cry!' What shall I cry? Let tears stream down day and night, O daughter of Zion. Lift your hands to him for the lives of your children."

"A Galilean accent," said one of the priests disdainfully.

"He is required to read from the law," objected a Levite, "but these are the words of prophets."

"It is odd the way he speaks," said the scribe as if to himself. "He is not reading. Neither is he quoting from memory like the illiterates." He strained to catch the boy's voice over the clamor of the temple.

"I hear the sound of a trumpet. He sits above the circle of the earth. Its inhabitants are like grasshoppers, the rulers of the earth are as nothing. You who oppress the poor and crush the needy, the days are coming when they shall take you away with hooks, even the last of you with fishhooks. All the birds of the air will settle on you."

The priests and Levites moved on, but the scribe stood for a moment and listened with a troubled look as the boy continued.

# 9

At the age of thirteen Jesus was apprenticed to his father, Yosef, learning the several crafts of building. From Nazareth they frequently traveled to the larger cities of Sepphoris and

Tiberias. There they built great houses for merchants, Roman officials, and priests.

Yosef oversaw the work of as many as twenty freemen and slaves: stonecutters, carpenters, hod carriers, tilers, masons, carvers.

During these times Jesus lived not with his father in the inn but in the huts of the slaves, where each night he slept on a nest of fetid hay. Paid less than the other apprentices, but just as subject to his father's hard discipline, he worked through the hours of daylight, sharing with the slaves their diet of gruel and dark bread. They never guessed he was the son of the builder.

Several times a day his father came to where Jesus was working and sighted the line of stones the boy had lain or pushed against the corners of the wood framing he had erected, testing their strength. He either nodded his silent approval or hit the boy in the legs with his staff, sometimes knocking him to the ground and waiting until he stood and finished his task correctly.

One day, during the building of a large villa for a quaestor in the Roman court, his father appeared with the owner to view the progress of the construction. The quaestor stopped to watch the masons placing stones in their fitted slots.

Yosef turned to an aging slave. "Put this stone here," he commanded.

The slave pushed his fingers under the stone and tried to raise it off the ground.

"Lift," he said. "Harder."

The old man managed to pull the stone up to his waist, halfway to the top of the wall.

"Higher."

The slave's chest was heaving with the exertion but he could raise it no further. Yosef struck him across the shoulders with his staff. The slave dropped the stone and fell with a cry to the ground.

"Stand," Yosef commanded.

The slave held his crushed foot and did not stand. His father struck him again, then again, until the cries of pain ceased. He ordered someone to pull the slave away. Strings of blood lay across the construction debris.

The quaestor looked down. "My house will be unclean," he said, "if this man's blood mixes with the mortar."

"Clean it up," his father said to Jesus.

Later in the day Jesus heard his father laugh at one of the owner's jests.

# 10

As they came of age, each of Jesus' brothers was apprenticed to their father. Absorbed by the task of training his younger sons, Yosef no longer examined the work of his eldest.

Jesus continued to work toward mastery in each of the crafts. He learned to decorate the entrance to a house, to attach roof tiles in straight lines, to lay marble floor slabs with precision. But increasingly he would pause in his work and gaze in silence at the ground or at the surrounding countryside.

One day he went to his father. "Give me my inheritance."

Yosef thought for a moment. "The amount of your inheritance is uncertain. Your brothers are sure to contest it. Instead I
will pay you the wages I held from you during your youth."

He counted out silver coins from his purse and gave them to
Jesus. He said nothing more. Jesus turned and left him.


# I I


He found Miryam in the courtyard of her house, sitting
motionless in the warmth of the sun.

"My father gave me the wages he owed me," he said and
showed her the silver coins.

She straightened and leaned back. "You are leaving, then."

"So you know."

"I know it from a dream. But it is an evil dream."

She closed her eyes. Jesus waited.

"There was a dazzling being. It was the sun with wings.
No, I saw as it came toward me it was a seraph. An eagle. No,
a hawk. Then a vulture. A dove. A sparrow. Then a fly, and
then nothing."

Slowly she opened her eyes and looked up at him. "When I
woke, I knew who the winged creature was. I knew you would
soon come to me and would soon begin your fall as in the dream."

Jesus stared at the earthen floor between them. "I must go."

Miryam rose to her feet. "You are too young. I will send
your brothers to bring you back."

Jesus shook his head. "I will not come with them."

"I send them only to protect you from evil."

"I know now there is no protection from evil. This is why I leave."

Miryam drew her breath as though to speak, but said nothing.

# 12

Jesus took flight up into the hill country of Ephraim. He passed his time alone and in silence except to exchange brief greetings with other wanderers and to beg for handfuls of grain and fruit from farmers working in their fields.

He walked slowly, turning this way and that. With a curious eye he surveyed the earth around him as though he were seeing it for the first time.

Once he stood until dark, gazing at a giant cedar standing in the center of a wheat field.

He followed the tracks of snails across the rocks before the morning dew dried on them. When the sun was full, he turned his attention to ants speeding through their labors, whistled at the chaffinch, and imitated the darting of the wagtail.

Occasionally he joined a small crowd of people following an itinerant rabbi, or a wonderworker, or a proselytizing insurrectionist.

His hair grew long. He slept in the open field or next to animals in their stalls. Threads hung loose from his cloak.

When his sandals rotted and broke, he kicked them off and went barefoot. He laughed often, at the creatures around him, at himself, at the endless speculations and arguments of the rabbis. Whoever passed him on the road stepped out of his way, taking him to be a madman.

# 13

Occasionally he spent days in the company of a wandering rabbi and his students, listening closely to the teachings and the arguments they seemed never to tire from.

"I plant an olive tree at the edge of my field," a rabbi asked, testing his students, "and after several years the tree grows large enough that it drops half its fruit on my neighbor's field. To whom does the fruit belong?"

"To the one who planted the tree," most of the students responded.

But one said, "To the neighbor."

"Why do you say so?" asked the rabbi.

"Whatever lies on my land belongs to me."

"What if your goat wanders onto your neighbor's field? Does it then belong to your neighbor?"

"If I did not tether it properly, yes. For then I would have treated the goat as though it did not belong to me."

"How then do you tether the olives that hang over your neighbor's field?"

"The olives drop onto my neighbor's field because they ripen or a wind has blown them. They are there by an act of God."

"Is God then mindful of the olives but not of the goat?" the rabbi asked.

So they talked through the day, even into the night, no more able to persuade each other than the stars they finally slept beneath.

# 14

Some of the rabbis used parables to hold the attention of their listeners. One of them told this story:

A rich man gave six silver coins to each of his three servants and sent them to the market, instructing them to buy wisely and to come home with goods that were the full value of the money.

But he didn't say what he wanted them to buy.

When the first reached the market, he was weak with hunger. His eye was drawn to nothing but food, especially to the costly oat bread and citrons. He bargained and bought them for a fair price. On the way home, now too hungry to walk, he ate one of the citrons and half the bread.

The second servant was attracted to a single pearl, the largest she had ever seen. She could not have it for less than nine silver coins, the merchant told her. When she offered him all six of her coins, he laughed at her, but she stood there, unable to go elsewhere. At the end of the day, the pearl remained unsold. Reluctantly, the merchant exchanged it for her six coins.

The third was cleverer still. He convinced a fool to gamble with him and to his six coins he added another six.

"Does the story end there?" one of the listeners asked.

"Yes."

"What is its meaning?"

"This is for you to discover," the storyteller said.

They agreed that the first servant was the most reckless, coming home with half the value of the six coins. The second increased the amount by half, but the third doubled it. On the other hand, the third was the most foolish of the three for he risked losing it all. As for the second, she could have worn the pearl as a jewel, greatly increasing the public esteem for the master's generosity. But what about the first servant?

For the first time, Jesus entered one of these discussions. "You are wrong about the first servant," he said. "If he had not eaten the bread, he would have starved and never returned. For three coins the master has his servant back. Who could measure the value of a servant?"

The listeners were surprised by this remark, saying nothing in response. When they turned to the storyteller to resolve the matter, he was not to be found.

# 15

One day Jesus joined an aged beggar walking with the aid of a stick. Together they scavenged a handful of dry spelt from a blowing grain field and several bunches of grapes from a vineyard that bordered the road. When they had eaten, they began to talk.

He told Jesus this story:

There was a certain man who acquired a modest wealth raising pigs. The man's wife died in childbirth and left him one son. The boy became a dutiful assistant to his father in managing his estate. When he came of age, the boy asked for his inheritance.

"I want to use the money to add to our wealth," the son said.

"You are young," his father said, "but a good worker. I will give you half your inheritance."

The young man set off boldly, his head full of dreams.

Weeks passed, then months. A year went by without a word, then years. The father believed the son was dead.

One day the steward came running to the father.

"Your son is back," he cried. "He asked for work feeding the swine."

He found his son standing in the muck and embraced him. "You are my son, but how changed. I would not have known you on the road."

He brought him into the house, listened to his long tale of misfortune, and with a full heart restored him to his place.

The father grew old. Knowing he would soon not be able to work the farm, he put his son in charge of it. The son quickly sold the land and the animals, and went to the city to multiply his wealth.

For a long time the old man was silent, then he added, "He has not been seen since."

"And the father has become a beggar," Jesus said.

"A beggar."

"You are that father."

"I am that father. How I wish I had never been. Twice I was made a fool for loving my son, my only child."

The old man spoke no more of these things.

Jesus said nothing but he did not forget.

# 16

Many were the stories he heard in the years of his wandering. Having little to say for himself, he listened in silence to the long accounts of misfortune others were ready to share.

With these stories in his heart he increasingly looked for solace in isolated country. Remembering how the ascetics spoke of the severe emptiness of the Judean desert, he walked south, following the river, leaving Galilee for the first time.

This journey began in the spring. Recent rains had raised the river's water. Only the largest rocks were visible, separated from each other by the dark torrents forking around them.

Coming to a narrow pass, Jesus climbed to the edge of a boulder and gazed down at the tumult.

"Stay! Take not another step!" came a voice from the other side.

A man, gaunt, nearly naked, his face hidden in a blowing mane of hair, was pointing at him.

"There is a fire coming that will eat the earth and all its people," he said, raising his voice above the sound of the river. "Even the waters of this river will burn like oil. Nothing can protect you from the flames but the righteousness of a pure heart."

The skins tied around the man's body and his long crooked staff were those of a wandering prophet. His eyes, showing through the hair, had the gleam of madness in them. Although he had not seen him in the many years since their boyhood together, Jesus knew the voice well.

"Yohanan!" Jesus reached out to him. "Give me the end of your staff."

"You stand at the edge of life," Yohanan yelled back at him. "You can return to the death that is in you or you can throw yourself onto the mercy of the one who is to come."

"Yohanan!"

"Hear my warning. I tell you, in a day, in a minute, the justifier will come and will pass through sinners like a scythe through the harvest. Those he doesn't save he will cut down with a terrible rage."

"Stand back!"

Jesus crouched and leapt across, but his feet slipped out from under him on the mossy face of the rock and he fell toward the water. Grabbing an edge of the rock with one hand, he raised the other to Yohanan.

Yohanan leaned down until he was face to face with Jesus. "You tempt the river," the prophet hissed. "But the river is hungry for your arrogance. Your life is no longer your own. You are being tested. Surrender."

He pried Jesus' hand loose with the butt of his staff. Jesus dropped backward into the current and disappeared.

He came to the surface below the rapids, his robe floating next to him like a severed wing. Drifting at the edge of an eddy, he was washed onto a delta of river grass.

When he had come to his feet, he looked back at Yohanan who was stretching his arms at the sky, a gesture of exultation.

Jesus turned and walked in the direction of the wilderness.

# 17

After the first pains of hunger had passed and the clarity had begun, he learned to find shelter during the middle of the day in a cave or in the shadow of a rock.

Now needing little sleep, he listened to the booming echoes of the wind along canyon walls and watched spirals of dust chasing each other through the wadis. At night the screeching of jackals was sometimes answered by the tremulous mourning of an owl.

"Surely these are signs," he said to himself and waited for the sounds to announce their meaning. "Show yourselves!" he demanded of the demons masked as whirling columns of sand. He studied the markings on the shells of beetles as though they were an occult code and wondered at the secret powers of the tiny dark plants that feed on stone.

The days passed until they could no longer be numbered, but what was hidden remained hidden.

Once, stretched out in the cool dark of a shallow cave, he sensed a movement in the rock above him. Another sign? No, he saw in a moment, only a small lizard.

He sprang to his feet, startled. It was not the lizard that startled him but something else. The animal was invisible, yet in full view. It was hidden but also plain to see.

He stepped into the sun. It was midday, hardly a shadow anywhere. The light left nothing unrevealed. Whatever was to be seen could be seen, if he but looked.

A raven, close enough that he noticed a dot of light in its eye, returned his gaze. He was the watcher watched. So was the raven.

The raven was not a sign, not an omen. Instead, something opened around them, something without boundary. What had opened was not behind the object seen; it was behind the seeing.

Jesus walked away, into the sunlight. The raven continued to hold him in its unmoving eye.

# 18

Because the moon was full he could continue his search for water into the night. He had searched for days.

There was light enough that he could see the edge of the promontory before him and the steep descent beyond it. A few dark trees were visible at the bottom of the gorge.

He stopped several times to trace his path downward. Though the wind was still, he thought he could hear a soft breathing among the rocks.

When he reached the bottom, he knelt and pressed down on a mossy patch of earth. A warm seep of water covered the back of his hand. He sucked at it until nothing was left, then turned to try another patch.

A foot came down firmly on his hand. He looked up. Gazing back at him was a tall young man dressed in the hooded cloak of a desert nomad. But his thick leather vest and iron-tipped spear were those of an insurrectionist.

Jesus pulled his hand free and sat back.

Shadows moved around them. Dark figures, similarly armed, rose from behind rocks and came slowly forward.

"Stand," he was ordered by the young man, obviously the commander of this rebel group. "You are a spy."

"Why do you say this?"

The commander pulled at Jesus' rags. "You disguise yourself as a beggar. Do you find many to beg from in the desert?" Someone laughed.

"Why would I beg when I have all that is necessary?"

"Would you beg for your life?"

"Why? Do you think life is necessary?"

"The Romans think it is—theirs, not ours."

"Then it is you who are the beggars."

"We beg for nothing," the commander exclaimed. "We will take what they will not give us."

"You would rather be Romans than Jews?"

"We would rather have what the Romans have taken from us."

"Have they taken your Jewishness from you?"

The commander hesitated. "Why do you say this?"

"A people that sees itself through the power of others is no longer a people."

"Hah! You think we are without power?"

"I think only that your hatred binds you to Rome."

"You are clever with words," the commander said. "But I see that you are also brave."

He held up the spear. Moonlight reflected off its iron point. "Will you be brave with this, or just clever? I give you a choice. Take this and go with us, or—surrender your life to it. Fight, or die."

Jesus said nothing.

"Silence will bring only death," the young man warned, and offered him the weapon.

Jesus did not move.

An owl sounded from the cliffs above them. The commander paused to listen. Again the owl sounded, now closer. The commander's face darkened. He turned to an old man standing behind him.

"Is this an omen?" he asked.

"It is certainly an omen," the old man replied. The owl sounded once more. "Release the prisoner," he said.

At a signal from the commander, the figures vanished back into the rocks as quickly and quietly as they had appeared.

Jesus fell to his knees and sucked at the damp soil.

# 19

One evening he stood at the summit of a rise watching the purple light obscure the hills around him.

Not for the first time, he heard his own voice in the windless void. He had been speaking out loud. As always, the words flew from him, forgotten as soon as they were said. With no one to hear, his tongue ran on unchecked. Thoughts were little more than scrambled sound.

"Elijah!"

The sound of the name alarmed him. Did this come from his own throat or was it the prophet announcing himself?

"Abraham!"

The name echoed through the space before him. But was he the listener or the speaker?

"El Shaddai!"

He sealed his lips. To block the rush of words rising from within, he tried to listen to the silence of the wilderness.

Instead he could hear only the known names of God, then the unknown names, one coming on top of another.

When they stopped, a hoarseness had seized his throat. He tried to utter his own name to the emptiness. But he did not have the breath for it. So the secret names returned, cried out by a voice to whom no speaker belonged.

With the first light of dawn, a quiet descended. Nothing was spoken and nothing was heard, all the names of God forgotten.

Softly, he breathed his own name. The time to leave the wilderness had come.

# 20

The river was nearly dry. Only shallow pools of green, fetid water appeared here and there among the rocks. Dizzy with thirst and hunger, Jesus walked up from the valley to the well that lies just outside the gate to the city of Jericho.

A woman in Samaritan dress was leaning into the well, pulling at the rope.

Jesus stood to the side.

Coils of rope had gathered at her feet before the bucket appeared. She poured a trickle of water into a jar, then looked over at him.

"I can see the thirst in you," she said.

"I have come far."

She glanced at the water jar. He quickly drank its small supply. He silently nodded his gratitude to her.

The woman, her face shaded by a head covering, said, "The thirst I see in you could not be satisfied by ten of these jars."

"I don't understand," Jesus said.

The woman did not respond but continued to gaze at him from the darkness of her shawl.

"What is this—thirst—you speak of?"

"You are seeking something that cannot be found," she said.

"How do you see this?"

"Men come to me, sometimes women too, for what they can find nowhere else. I can give them what they long for. In you there is a longing that goes beyond all human comfort. I have much to give, rabbi, but not to you."

"Why do you call me 'rabbi'?"

"Because of what you have to teach."

Jesus stood for a moment in silence. "I? What do I have to . . . teach?"

"Your thirst."

A sudden gust blew sand against them with stinging force.

"Teach us your thirst," the woman said to him, "and we will find water where we could not expect it."

Jesus slowly shook his head, as if he were unsure of the meaning of her words.

"But first," she said, putting the bucket in his hands, "see what you can get from this well." A smile seemed to pass across her shaded face.

When he had filled her water jar, he went with her into Jericho.

# 21

"You have been in the wilderness," the Samaritan woman said to him.

He had stepped out of the sun and put down the water jar to rest. "Yes."

"I can see it from your weakness." She lightly brushed the loose threads of his sleeve. "And from these clothes."

Jesus looked down at the remains of his cloak.

The woman came closer.

"From the expression in your face," she said, "I can see you have been a wanderer. You have long been without a home."

"Years. How many, I don't remember."

"You will leave every home others make for you."

"How do you know this of me?"

She lifted back the shawl so he could see her face in the light. He gazed at her in silence. It was long before she spoke.

"You are surprised by what shows in me."

"There is much that surprises me," he said.

She nodded at the water jar. He lifted it to his shoulder and walked after her.

# 22

Not long after this, they passed a small group of students with their teacher, an aging priest. When Jesus saw how they turned away from her and whispered to each other, he stopped.

"They scorn you," he said.

"Yes."

Jesus spoke to the teacher. "By what authority do you judge this woman?"

"This woman God judges," the teacher replied.

"Are you God that you can know the heart of another?"

"I know and live by the laws of God," the teacher said. "You cannot embrace this woman and also embrace the divine law."

The students looked silently into the face of Jesus. Behind them others stopped to listen.

"Is there a law of God that forbids our love for any created being?" Jesus asked the teacher.

"God commands us to shun what is unclean."

"If God commands this, it is God's to command, not yours."

The teacher looked down at Jesus' tattered robe and his naked feet. "Are you a rabbi that you presume to teach us the law?"

"He is a rabbi," said the woman, "who has much to teach. Listen to him."

"And shall I listen to you as well?" the teacher asked.

"Those you judge," Jesus said to the teacher, "you must listen to most of all."

The old priest drew in his cloak so as not to touch Jesus and the woman, and led his students through the surrounding crowd. No one else moved.

Jesus felt a hand on his arm. A paralytic, his twisted body supported by a child, was reaching out to him.

Jesus looked from the paralytic to the woman. When she said nothing, he held up his hands to the paralytic, showing he could do nothing for the man's condition, and walked from the market.

The crowd followed for a way.

# 23

Days later, sitting in the shade at the edge of the market, Jesus caught sight of the paralytic and the child as they made their way through the crowd, begging and receiving nothing.

They came to Jesus and asked him for food. He took bread from his pouch and divided it with them.

"You came to me before," Jesus said, "but it was not to beg."

"I heard your voice," the paralytic answered, "and knew you had the power of healing. I reached for your hand because I wanted to walk again. You would not touch me."

"I do not have the power to straighten your legs," Jesus said.

"You have a greater power, rabbi," said the paralytic.

Jesus was silent.

"You looked at me but it was without pity and without compassion," the paralytic continued. "When you didn't touch me, I saw that you too have a need for healing."

The paralytic held up the last crust of his bread. "You didn't give us your food. You ate it with us."

"What is your name?" Jesus asked.

"Nathanael."

"And yours?" he said to the child.

"She doesn't remember her name," Nathanael said. "I call her Havah."

The paralytic pointed toward the market. "I have told many about you."

# 24

Later that day when they had eaten, Jesus asked, "Why do the people come to me?"

"They are in need," the Samaritan woman answered. "They look everywhere for leaders."

"And everywhere," Jesus replied, "there are leaders to be found. I have met them on the roads: priests, wizards, baptizers, wonderworkers, ascetics, messiahs, Pharisees, caesars. All of them looking for followers."

"These do not lead. They replace one bondage with another."

"I have nothing to promise the people, no worldly substance to draw them," Jesus said looking down at the sparrows pecking at the dust around them. "I can't even feed these birds."

"Food is what others promise. They can lead only when the people are in want."

"Many are in want."

"Thus the power of their rulers."

"There is a deeper want," Jesus said. "The people still are not fed."

"There is only one food for this greater hunger."

Jesus waited.

"It is what you saw in the raven's eye," she said.

He shook his head. "What I saw in the raven's eye is not to be given. It is already there."

"It is not what they receive from you but what they see in you that draws them."

"I don't understand."

"Look," she said.

A small crowd was coming toward them led by the paralytic and the child.

Jesus turned and walked away. The Samaritan woman stood for a moment then joined him.

# 25

Jerusalem's walls came into view as they continued up the road. The great temple, reflecting the afternoon sun, rose above the walls like a divine warning.

They walked in silence. The road was busy with merchants, pilgrims, beggars, soldiers, farmers leading a few sheep or a goat to the market, and the great shuffling army of wanderers with neither home nor destination.

At the edge of the city a luminescent stream of sewage poured into an extended sump of offal and rotting trash. A ring of small fires left a veil of sulphuric smoke hanging in the windless air, obscuring the figures, mostly children, picking through the rubbish.

To a small girl searching through animal feces for grain Jesus offered a piece of the loaf hidden in his cloak. She looked up with terror, backed away, and presently resumed her labor.

# 26

They passed through the Dung Gate into the city and its clamor of people and noise. The Samaritan woman, familiar with the streets, led Jesus through narrow alleys to the temple mount.

Armed and uniformed temple guards lined the grand stairway that led to the courtyard and entrance. In the area surrounding the temple scores of healers, wonderworkers, and prophets competed with each other for the attention of the restless throng.

Jesus and the Samaritan caught sight of the tall figure of the baptizer, his halo of reddish hair visible at a distance. Closer, they could hear his maledictions, called out in a voice worn rough from shouting.

"This city will be rent by the vengeful hand of God," he bellowed, "each side inflamed and blinded by false righteousness."

He was surrounded by a small band of enthusiasts. A larger crowd of idlers listened briefly and wandered on. A line of temple guards kept a bored eye on the baptizer.

"The rivers of filth that pour down from her walls will be cleansed with the blood of the wicked dying at the hands of the wicked. But the filth that streams from their darkened minds will but call up a greater pestilence."

Yohanan gazed upward then closed his eyes, the sun full in his face.

"But will God leave his people unprotected from themselves?" he called out. "No, I tell you. No. He will send one as yet unknown, a warrior of the spirit, hammer of heaven, to slay the wickedness in the hearts of all of us."

As the baptizer continued, scarcely pausing for breath, Jesus drew closer, the Samaritan woman following. Softly, Jesus spoke the name of his kinsman. Yohanan spun toward him. His glance fell on the woman, then he studied Jesus' tattered cloak. He seized Jesus and turned him to face the crowd.

"This one!" he cried. "Observe him well—child of sin, fatherless, conceived against the commandments, his heart not yet cleansed of impurity." An animal gleam came into Yohanan's eyes. "But I have witnessed his surrender. He is a soldier of God. Follow him. His name will be on the tongues of those who kill for righteousness' sake. But he will not live out the year. He will go unseen to a forgotten grave. In his wake the evil forces will attack each other in fury."

He guided Jesus into the midst of the people then raised his hands to heaven. Jesus quickly slipped away and passed through the stunned onlookers.

He followed the Samaritan through a maze of narrow alleys until they reached the well of Siloam where they joined those gathered there for its healing waters.

"How am I to understand what Yohanan said?" Jesus asked her.

"Because he is acquainted with the hatred in the hearts of others," she answered, "he is a true prophet. Listen to him. But do not do as he says. Like all prophets, his own hatred remains hidden from him."

# 27

Taking one of the fragments of pottery lying at the edge of the well, Jesus reached deep into the opening, brought up a small quantity of dark water, and gave it to the woman. When he had taken some himself, they started up the steps, finding their way through the noisy crowd of those gathered there to seek healing or to beg.

A woman pulled his cloak. A child lay listless in her arms.

"Rabbi, bless my child."

"What is her illness?"

"She is hungry," the woman said. "She has had nothing but a few scraps of bread for many days and now is so weak she will not even drink water from the well."

Jesus put his hand on the child. She brightened and looked up at him, but soon she leaned back and the light left her eyes.

Near them, seated on the ground, was a man in rags whose legs were badly twisted. He touched their feet and held up an empty hand.

Jesus knelt and asked the man about his illness.

"It is not an illness that brought me here," he said. "I was a stonemason and was injured. I am now too weak to do the only work I know."

When the man saw that Jesus had nothing to give him, he drew back and reached toward the foot of another, his hand still open and empty.

There were others: a boy with no legs who shuffled strangely on his hands, a woman who was cruelly jerked and thrown by an inner demon, a man who said he was the emperor Caesar, commanding the ants about him as though they were legions, a child too despondent to push away the dog licking his sores.

"I feel the strength going out of me," Jesus said to the woman. She led him up to the street.

# 28

They passed the entrance of a small synagogue as the congregation, animated and talking rapidly, emptied into the street. There was a young Pharisee in their midst. It was to him that most of the questions were addressed.

When Jesus and the Samaritan woman heard the Pharisee's voice, they stopped. He spoke quietly and without haste but with an authority that silenced his listeners.

"How can it be, as you say, that nothing should come before the study of torah?" he was asked.

"If there is something that comes before torah," he replied, "then study that."

"But my family would starve if I placed torah before the few coins I am able to earn from my work."

The rabbi stood in silence for a moment. When he had their attention, he told this story:

There was once a young student who earned no more than one zuz a day, barely enough to keep himself alive. Nonetheless, he gave half of it to the guard at the house of study so he could be admitted to hear the reading of torah; the other half he shared with his family.

Once, on a cold winter day, he heard that a famous rabbi was to read torah. Unable to work because of the weather, he earned nothing that day. When no amount of begging would get him into the house of study, he secretly climbed onto the roof where he could hear the rabbi through the skylight.

While he was there it snowed and grew so cold he was unable to move.

The next day was sabbath. The sun came up brightly but the house of study remained dark. It was thus that the student was discovered frozen to the skylight.

When they asked the famous rabbi what they were to do, for the sabbath laws forbade their climbing onto the roof, he severely reproved them.

"What?" he cried. "Does torah come from the sabbath or the sabbath from torah? Just as this young man's love of torah places him far above the floor of the house of study so does it place him far above the sabbath. Rescue him. The sabbath was made for labor like this."

They climbed to the roof at once, lowered the student through the opening, and put him before a hot fire until life returned to him.

The people seemed unsatisfied with this answer. They remained standing where they were and pressed the young Pharisee with more questions.

In an aside, the Samaritan said to Jesus, "He is himself the boy he speaks about."

"Is there an end to the study of torah?" one asked. "How do we know when our study has been sufficient?" asked another. "How do we know when we have understood what is written?"

"You will have studied enough," the Pharisee said, "when you know exactly what torah says."

"You are a teacher. Can't you tell us what it says?"

"It is so simple I could tell it to you while standing on one foot."

"Do that! Stand on one foot. Tell us!"

"If I told you, you would still not know. You must find it yourself, in your own study."

"Can we find it in torah?"

"Your life will lead you to it while studying torah."

When he saw that they were puzzled, he told them this story:

There once was a student who wanted to learn the essential teachings of torah. He was given the name of three famed rabbis, one greater than the other. He went immediately to the house of the first. When he arrived he found the family in grief; the rabbi had just died.

When he found the house of the second rabbi, he was greeted there too with the cries of mourning.

One name remained, that of the greatest of the three. With dread the student made his way to the door of the third. It was the rabbi himself who answered his knock.

"Yes?"

"I want to learn the essential teachings of torah," the student explained timidly.

"Why this look on your face?" the rabbi asked. "Are you so afraid of what I might teach you?"

The student told him what had happened.

"Then I cannot be your teacher," the great rabbi answered. "I can add nothing to what you have already learned from the first two rabbis."

There was a clamor of voices as they asked still more questions. But the Pharisee said nothing. He was looking beyond
them at Jesus and the woman. It was a look so solemn the
people followed his gaze. They saw only a barefoot beggar and
his companion.

"You understand then, rabbi," he said to Jesus.

"Yes. I understand."

As Jesus and the woman walked away, the people asked,
"Why did you call him 'rabbi'?"

"I saw from his face that this was his story, too."

# 29

Standing before them were Nathanael and Havah.

"We followed you here," Nathanael said. "We are not alone."

Behind him was a cluster of curious faces. As Jesus looked
up at them, they drew closer and spoke their names.

They were Didymos, a scribe; Avisgai, a ruined priest; a
gaunt, scarred youth who had the appearance of a fugitive soldier and refused to give his name; a certain Eliezer bar Shimon
who said he was a chazzan in the synagogue at Capernaum, on a
pilgrimage to Jerusalem; Devorah, the widow of a wealthy
landowner; Zakkai, who said nothing of himself, but was
leading an idiot by a rope tied to his wrist—"He can't say a
word, not even his name—Bartholomew"; and Yaakov, who
concealed his hands in his robe as the lepers do.

Others stood at a greater distance.

"These saw you with the baptizer," Nathanael said, "and they too are ready to follow."

"How can they follow when I have no place to lead them?"

"They want only to be your people and will go wherever you go."

"My people?" Jesus said. "Can't they see that no one belongs to me?"

Nathanael threw open his hands and said nothing.

Jesus thought for a moment. "Come, then."


# 30

Not long after this, Nathanael led a blind man to Jesus.

"I explained to him," Nathanael said, "that you have the powers of a healer. This man expressed a great desire for healing and was eager to come to you."

Jesus spoke directly to the blind man. "I do not have the power to restore your eyes."

"You do not understand, rabbi," he said in a whisper, his fingers playing over Jesus' face. "I already see, rabbi. It is the others who do not see."

"Are you not blind, then?"

"Although I was born without eyes, rabbi, I have never lived in darkness. Mine is a world of a thousand dimensions and colors. I hear and smell and touch all that you do but in hues and shapes unknown to anyone else."

Jesus stared into his empty eye sockets.

"Were King Herod to behold what I see for half a day, he would trade all he has for such wealth."

"If you do not suffer," Jesus asked him, "why did you come to me to be healed?"

"I suffer from the blindness of others. Wherever I go, rabbi, I find those who have never seen but do not know they are sightless. Everywhere I find those whom the sightless never notice; and they, too, are often unseeing."

Jesus said nothing.

"I did not come to you to be healed. It is the unseeing who need to be healed."

"What is your name?"

"Levi."

"Come with us."

# 31

A tall, graying man stopped at a short distance from Jesus and his friends. He was dressed in the robe of a pagan philosopher. A small leather bag was attached to the end of his staff.

He drew aside two members of the group. "This teacher," he said, "is he in possession of the truth?"

"As for truth, we know little," Didymos answered. "We know only that when he speaks his words come to life in our hearts."

"Then you are his disciples."

"He calls us his friends but we call each other his disciples."

"The leper also?"

"The leper also."

"Even the women?"

"Yes."

The philosopher drew closer, gave his name as Judas, and recited the lineage of his teachers. "I am not a teacher but I will share what I understand, however little, with anyone who listens, however great." He drew in his breath and leaned toward them. "I have conversed with the governor himself, Pilatus."

Didymos looked up at the philosopher with a doubtful expression.

"He has commanded me to learn the teaching of the Judean sages that I might share their wisdom with him." He tapped the leather bag at the end of his staff. "This contains my entire earthly wealth—nothing more than the small salary the governor has given me."

In spite of Judas' boast, Didymos noted that the philosopher's eyes had the clear light of honesty in them.

"What are the guiding ideas of your master's teaching?" Judas asked.

"He can tell you better himself. He is standing there."

Judas stepped before Jesus and planted his staff in the dust. He straightened and looked down from his superior height. "I am a wandering philosopher who dwells in no earthly home, but only in that truth where all knowledge is one. I seek a teacher whose words will illumine the path before me."

Jesus took note of his robe. "You are not a believer."

"I am not a believer."

"Your disbelief is precious to you."

"It is the food and breath of my seeking," Judas responded.

"If you lost your disbelief," Jesus said, "you would lose . . ."

"Everything. My life."

"You are privileged, Judas. Because you are prepared to lose everything, you understand faith. Come with us, then."

# 32

Early the next morning Jesus rose before the others. He glanced over their sleeping forms. Exhausted by hunger, they would wake slowly.

He knelt next to the Samaritan and spoke quietly to her. When she saw that he was ready to leave, she stood and went with him.

After they had walked a while, she said, "You ask the people to come. Still, you don't know why they follow."

"Like them," Jesus said, "I have no path."

"They see that no one leads you. They see you have no need of followers. I hear them talk with each other. They say, 'He has a divine spirit.'"

"Can't they see?"

The Samaritan said nothing to this.

"They call me 'rabbi' but with what words am I to teach them?"

"Stories. As you often do with me."

"Stories? The stories come from . . . I don't know where. And many I don't understand myself."

"Then the stories will be the teacher."

Jesus could not see her face but there was a smile in her voice when she said this.

"Wait here," she said. They waited until the others joined them.

# 33

On the road down from Jerusalem, north toward Gibeah, Jesus entered into a long silence. His friends ceased speaking with each other. The Samaritan woman was walking behind him. Hours passed. Even the hills seemed to have entered the circle of quiet.

Didymos walked with him for a while and was the first to break the silence. "You speak so little," he said, "but there is so much to know. I try to remember each of your words."

"Forget my words. It is what you say because of them that matters."

When Jesus saw that Didymos was puzzled, he told this story:

In a time of drought a man borrowed two seah of barley from a neighbor to feed his family. A small amount remained. He planted it.

The next year he went to pay back the barley but his neighbor said his crop was sufficient. So the farmer planted the barley again, calculating carefully how much it had expanded in that harvest.

The next year the same exchange occurred between the farmer and his neighbor, and several years after that.

Five years passed and the neighbor still prospered. But one day a second neighbor came to the farmer with the news that his crop had failed and he was in need of help. The farmer sent this second neighbor ten wagons overflowing with barley.

# 34

"I often see laughter in your eyes," Jesus said to the Samaritan. "I saw it first at the well."

They were seated in the thin shade of trees that had taken root at a turn of the river. A small crowd had gathered around them, some sleeping, others awake with the empty stare of hunger.

"I see it now, again," he said.

"Yes," she said. "I am full of laughter."

"How can that be? These people who follow us—they are in such need. Starving, broken, without hope. But you can still laugh."

"Laughter is the door to sadness. Whoever cannot laugh cannot know the depth of their grief. Those who are not full of laughter cannot see they are also full of hatred."

"Hatred?"

"Yes," she said, "there is much to hate."

"I find little laughter in myself."

"Rabbi, your words float on it. They lead the words of others as though in a dance."

"But I myself wait for the words," Jesus said. "I, too, follow them, unsure where they lead."

"See. This is the dancing I speak of."

Jesus laughed.


# 35

Some days later, as they made their way into the town of Cana, a rich man seeing the procession presented himself to Jesus. Behind him servants carried his son on a litter.

"I have been to many wonderworkers," the man said, holding up a fat purse, "offering them more money than they will see in a lifetime if they can heal my son."

Jesus looked down at the man's son. His arms and legs were

fleshless as a bird's. The boy stared back at him with fear in his eyes. Jesus leaned over.

"I cannot heal you," he said quietly to the boy. "You don't need to be healed. There is a strength in your illness. Find it. Live by it."

The boy's father, hearing none of this, said in a loud voice, "What? You won't heal him? Aren't miracles possible to those who believe?"

"I can perform no miracles," Jesus said to him.

The man replied with anger, "Do these people follow you for nothing?"

"If miracles are everything, yes, they follow me for nothing."

The man told his servants to move on. Then he saw that the litter was empty.

"Where's my son?" he cried.

"The boy got up," the servants told him, "and disappeared into the crowd."

In panic, the man flew into the street calling out the boy's name, leaving Jesus, the servants, and the money behind.


# 36


Passing through the busy center of Cana, Jesus caught sight of a child darting through the crowd as though looking for a place to hide.

When she came to where he was standing with his friends, she slid behind him and covered her face with his cloak.

"What is it you want?" he asked her.

"Protect me," she gasped. "The soldiers are looking for me."

"What did you do?"

She hesitated. "I took bread from the baker."

"Where is it?"

"I ate it."

"Don't hide," he said, as the soldiers approached. "Stand next to me and say nothing."

"Did you see a thief running this way?" the soldiers asked people in the crowd. They looked down as they walked, saying nothing.

Then the soldiers came to Jesus.

"Yes," Jesus answered. "I saw your thief."

"Did you see her well? Could you describe her?"

"Yes. She is thin, arms and legs like sticks, hungry, ill-dressed, and frightened."

The soldiers looked about. "Everybody could be so described."

"Then you have found your thief."

The soldiers glanced at him with scorn and walked away.

Jesus turned to the girl. He saw that she was not as young as he thought. "What is your name?"

"Martha."

"Do you have a home?"

She stared at the dust around her feet. "When my father died, I had to leave. He was a rabbi." She paused, then added, "I can read."

"Come with us, Martha," Jesus said.

# 37

After leaving the city on the main road along the Lake of Galilee, they were overtaken by a stream of people, some in groups, some walking singly, racing on ahead.

"Where are you going?" someone asked. "And why so fast?"

"Givrona the Judean, the healer and wonderworker, has come to the town just ahead. She has called the people to her. There are certain to be miracles!"

Soon they came to where the people were gathered on a hillside. Several gasped at the size of the crowd. "Five thousand," cried Didymos. "Even more."

The crowd formed a semicircle around a decorated tent. Before the tent lay scores of the ill, the crippled, the tormented. Presently one of Givrona's attendants emerged from the tent, stood before the crowd, and raised his hands to silence them.

When there was quiet everywhere, the entrance to the tent flew open and Givrona emerged: a tall woman with waist-length silver hair, draped in a brilliant red robe. Slowly and in awe the crowd began chanting her name. Many were in tears. Soon the chant became a wild shouting. Thousands reached out, pleading for her healing touch.

Givrona swept through the rows of invalids brushing each with a feather wand. Then she stood immobile, her face to the heavens. Once more a hush came over the crowd and they could hear her speaking a strange language, appealing to unseen powers.

Jesus looked on in silence. Some of those with him joined the throng.

Several were walking away from the crowd. Among them was a scribe named Joram. When he passed some of Jesus' friends, they asked why he was leaving. "This is a false wonder-worker," he answered. "She has no wonders to perform."

"Our teacher," said Nathanael, nodding toward Jesus, "has a true power of healing."

"This is your teacher—wearing such rags?"

"Observe him. You will see miracles."

As Nathanael spoke, Jesus and the Samaritan stopped to talk with a young man sitting with his wife and child at the edge of the road. Joram paused to listen.

The young man's wife, a child herself, was holding her breast to the mouth of the infant and staring away from the visitors. They had fashioned a rough shelter for themselves and it was now their only home, the man explained. They had been driven off their farm for slow repayment of their debt to local moneylenders.

"We have long been hungry," he said, "and now we are sick as well."

"Have you taken the child to Givrona?" Jesus asked.

The man nodded. "She touched us but the powers did not. She promised the child would be healed by the milk of life. But no such milk has come."

Jesus then noticed that the child was dead.

"So we remain here," the young father said, "hoping those who come to see the wonderworker would have pity on us. But they have their own illnesses."

Jesus knelt before the infant. "If I had the power, I would breathe life into her. But there is no such power."

The young mother turned toward Jesus, her face dark with fury.

As Jesus walked away, Joram went with him.

Several in the crowd were looking on. "Did you hear what

he said?" one of them asked the others. "He has the power to breathe life into the dead."

These, too, followed.

# 38

When Jesus saw that some of the sick and the lame rose from their pallets and took up their crutches to come toward him, he quickly led the Samaritan away. Only his friends and a few others went with him.

He walked all that day, not resting until he was sure none of those in need of healing could find him. He remained silent until it was dark and the others had folded themselves into their cloaks against the night chill.

Several, not understanding why Jesus fled the crowd, spoke among themselves. "He said he does not have the power to heal," one said, "but what of Nathanael who was once crippled but walks as well as any of us?"

"How can you say Nathanael is healed?" answered another. "Don't you see that he still holds on to his child?"

"Did he not heal the rich man's son who leapt from his pallet and ran into the city?"

"But if he healed the boy, what has he done for Yaakov? Has he cured his leprosy?"

"Has he cured my blindness?" Levi said in a soft voice. They stopped and looked at him. "I am blind but I am not sick with blindness. Neither is Yaakov sick with his leprosy. Why would he heal those who are not sick?"

"Didn't he heal the rich man's son?"

"He did something greater than healing," the blind man said.

"What can be greater than healing?"

"He freed the boy of the need to be healed." Levi saw they didn't understand. "If there was an illness in the boy's body," he explained, "there was a greater illness in the father's request. To do what the father asked could only make the illness worse."

No one accepted Levi's explanation and the argument continued.

# 39

Later Devorah went to Jesus where he was talking with the Samaritan. She told him what they had discussed.

"You say you don't have the power to heal," she said, "but they saw the boy rise and run off. Isn't this a wonder?"

"I can perform no wonders. Neither can anyone else. The wonders are always there before we come to them."

"How can that be?"

"Sit here, Devorah," he said, then told this story:

When the entire month of Adar passed without rain, the people went to a wonderworker begging him to pray for rain. He was reluctant.

"Rain? There is nothing to that," he said. "There are greater wonders."

The people said rain was all the wonder they could ever want. He finally agreed and sent them away. The rain soon came in great torrents and the people rejoiced. But the rain continued and they were unable to go into their fields and plant. The fields flooded, rich soil washed into swollen rivers.

They returned to the wonderworker. "Please end the rain. Bring the sun back," they pleaded with him, "even if this is a greater wonder."

Again the wonderworker was reluctant. Again the people prevailed. Soon the sun appeared and the people rejoiced. They went into the fields and planted their crops. But the sun was relentless. The young plants withered and died. Once more they went to the wonderworker.

"What do you want now?"

"Could you make it as it was before?" the people beseeched him.

"I told you there was a greater wonder," he answered them, "than those you asked for. This I cannot give you nor can I take it from you."

"What is this greater wonder?"

"It is that you do not want what you want."

"Why is this a wonder?" the people asked.

"Because if it were not so, you would learn nothing. You would see only what is necessary, not what is possible."

# 40

Coming near the city of Sepphoris, they met a small crowd of people loudly bargaining with each other.

Several priests, two Roman officials, and a number of prosperous citizens were bidding for a family of slaves. Soon they learned that all six members of the family were barbarians captured by soldiers in a warring province to the north and sold to one of the merchants from the town. Hoping to multiply his investment, the merchant was offering them singly to buyers.

The slaves were naked and bound at the neck, their mouths stuffed with rags tied from behind.

Jesus and his friends watched as the children, weakened by hunger and mistreatment, were sold at a lowered price. Their pleased owners pulled them off while those remaining clamored for the adults. Soon they too were sold and the crowd dispersed.

That evening, they made a fire at the opening to a cave above the city and ate in silence. Here and there they could see the flames of lanterns and candles in the larger homes and palaces. Voices of revelers echoed off the walls.

For a long time no one spoke. Then Havah said, "What will happen to the children?"

"Like you," Nathanael replied, "they may never see their parents again."

"Why," the child asked, "are there slaves?"

"Who could imagine the world without them?" said Eliezar bar Shimon. When Havah looked at him doubtfully, he added, "There is no law for this. It is lawful even for rabbis to have slaves."

Then Jesus spoke to them. "It is true that there is no law to free the slaves," he said, "but until they are free our obedience to every law is incomplete."

"How can this be?" Eliezar answered. "Am I to be judged for a law I never broke?"

Jesus carefully laid a handful of sticks on the fire and told this story:

A spelt merchant hired an assistant to help him in his expanding business. "I selected you because you are known for your honesty."

Over the years, he had many chances to test the servant's faithfulness. Never did the servant take so much as a single zuz that was not his, nor a handful of grain.

It was discovered, however, that the merchant had all this time been using false scales to steal from those who bought from him. He was brought to trial with his assistant.

"I find both of you guilty," the judge declared. "But you," he said, pointing to the assistant, "will serve a greater sentence."

"Why should I be punished more severely than my master?" the assistant protested. "I have not taken so much as a single zuz more than I was due."

"I know you are a perfectly honest man," the judge said. "Therefore you are the guiltier, for your morality hid an immorality."

# 41

The next day Jesus and his friends came to the village of Capernaum.

In addition to the Samaritan woman and the chazzan Eliezar, they were the fallen priest, Avisgai; the blind man, Levi; a grits dealer named Moshe; Didymos; Zakkai and Bartholomew; Judas; the widow Devorah and a companion; the leper Yaakov; Martha; the Jebusite soldier; Nathanael with Havah; and Joram the scribe.

A patrol of Roman soldiers was gathered at the gate to the village. Seeing the small band approach, they were suspicious and moved to block their way.

The Samaritan walked steadily forward, Jesus following, ignoring the soldiers' commands. They collided with a wall of shields.

"What reason have you for standing in our way?" Jesus asked the captain.

"What reason have you for disobeying our commands?" the captain answered loudly.

"If you had no weapons and no armor, you would not have commanded us," Jesus said.

The captain brushed the blade of his sword with his fingertips.

"You have surrendered your voice to your weapons," Jesus said. "Since iron has no words, your weapons say nothing. So we heard no commands. How can we surrender to that which cannot command?"

"Then whom do you obey?" the captain asked, pushing Jesus backward with the handle of his sword.

"We search for wisdom. We go wherever it summons us."

Smiling, the captain rested the blade of his sword on the naked edge of Jesus' shoulder. "And wisdom, does it not go where the sword leads it?"

Jesus reached into the bag at his side and removed a barley seed which he placed in his open hand. Then he picked up a small round stone. The captain watched him without speaking.

"The seed," Jesus said, "does it not obey the stone?" He ground the stone in his hand until the seed was dust. The captain nodded a reluctant assent.

Then Jesus drew another seed from the bag and knelt before the captain. Making a small depression in the earth with his hand, he carefully placed the seed in it, spit on it several times, and covered it with sand. The soldiers circled in closer to see what the rabbi had done.

"To whom will the earth belong, Captain?" Jesus gazed toward a gathering of villagers observing them. "Those who crush the seed or those who plant it?"

The captain made a menacing gesture with the sword.

Jesus tossed a handful of seed at the feet of the soldiers. They stepped back. He stamped gently on the exposed seeds and tossed out another handful. As the soldiers moved away to avoid trampling on the seeds, Jesus and his friends passed slowly through them and into the village of Capernaum.

# 42

Later that day the chazzan of the synagogue in Capernaum came to the town well where Jesus was sleeping in the sun next to the Samaritan. A tall, serious student was in the company of the chazzan. The student's name was Thaddeus.

When Jesus woke, the chazzan said, "I told the rabbi what you said to the Romans at the gate when you entered and he said, 'I must talk with this Jesus.' You and your friends are invited to come this evening to the house of study."

Jesus thought for a moment then indicated his assent.

Before Jesus could answer, Thaddeus took the sleeve of the chazzan and pulled him aside.

"How can we invite this man to eat with the rabbi if he brings such friends as these? One is a leper, another a Samaritan. That one is an idiot and that one has the scars of a soldier. How do we know they are not unclean? Even this Jesus seems unclean."

The chazzan listened patiently.

"Will they all come?" Thaddeus continued. "Will the women come with them?"

"You know how boldly he spoke to the soldier," the chazzan said. "How can we expect him to come without his friends?"

The student said nothing more. The chazzan turned to Jesus and his friends.

"We will come," Jesus said.

That evening they assembled in the house of study. In addition to Jesus and some of his friends, there were the rabbi and the rabbi's students. Like Thaddeus before them, some of the students appeared offended by the presence of the unclean. The rabbi ignored them.

When they had reclined, preparing to eat, the rabbi turned to Jesus. "I am told you deny that anyone can perform wonders. Didn't Moshe make his staff into a serpent when he cast it down before the pharaoh? Didn't Elijah restore a dead child to life?"

"It is written that God performed these wonders through Moshe and Elijah," Jesus answered, "but where does torah promise that you and I can use this power?"

"How else are we to understand these writings?"

"Why must we understand them at all?"

"What?" the rabbi exclaimed. "Torah is beyond under-standing?"

"What we can understand we don't need torah to learn."

The rabbi laughed and looked about him. The people were silent. The house of study was filled. They were about thirty in number.

"It is written," the rabbi said, "that God gave Moshe the law, but where is it written that God withheld Moshe's under-standing of it?"

"How are we to make sense of God?" Jesus laughed too and raised his cup to be filled. "It is also written that God sent Moshe back to Egypt to free the people of Israel then came at night and tried to kill him. Where is it written what God meant by this?"

"This is a difficult text," the rabbi admitted, "but surely you and I can come to an agreement on its meaning."

Jesus shrugged and told this story:

A millet farmer suggested to his neighbor, a vintner, that they buy an olive tree, splitting the cost evenly. The vintner agreed. They planted it on the boundary line between their properties.

The first year the vintner pruned half the tree, reducing the crop on his side almost to nothing. The following year, however, the pruned part of the tree produced double the remainder and grew larger than the other half.

When the millet farmer saw this, he asked the vintner to share half the produce.

"But I pruned my half and took the loss the first year," the vintner said.

"Who said it was your half? We bought it together. We mixed our money, why not our olives?"

"I should be recompensed for my labor in pruning."

"You were," the farmer said, "by having less labor in harvesting the first year."

"It was my idea to prune one side," the vintner argued. "It is because you didn't have this idea yourself that you have fewer olives."

"It was my idea to buy the tree. It is because I had this idea that you have any olives at all."

"Still, the pruned side hangs over my land."

"Does the rain fall only on your land?" the farmer asked. "Does the sun reach only half the tree? Are the roots divided also?"

"You could always prune your side," said the vintner.

"Your side will always be larger," the farmer answered.


Jesus paused, as though waiting for the vintner and the farmer to continue. But the listeners joined the argument, some taking one side, some the other. After a while they turned to Jesus.

"Who has the stronger argument?" they asked.

"Neither."

"Then how does the argument end?"

"Why should it end?"

There were many voices speaking at once. The rabbi raised his hand to silence them, then turned to Jesus. "We were talking about interpreting torah. Are you saying agreement is not possible?"

"Whenever we agree on the meaning of torah," Jesus responded, "that agreement takes the place of torah."

# 43

In the silence that followed this remark, there were many troubled faces. The widow Devorah seemed especially perturbed.

"If God's commands aren't clear," she asked, "how can we obey them?"

"The words of torah," Jesus answered, "do not tell us how we are to profit from their use."

"God doesn't know what he wants us to do with his own words?"

"The giver of these words can only be surprised by what we do with them."

When he saw they were waiting for more explanation, he told this story:

A master sent three servants to the market with six silver coins apiece, expecting them to use the money cleverly and to bring back something of greater value than the six coins.

One bought a jewel that was worth two times what the merchant thought. "I sold the jewel to another and have come back with twelve coins." The master praised her.

The second bought a goat he discovered was pregnant with two kids. "I felt the belly when the merchant was not looking. He thought I was buying one goat but I knew I was buying three. So I have tripled your six coins."

"You, too, have been most clever."

The third said, "I lost the coins."

"How could you be such a fool?" the master said.

"I came upon a group of itinerant performers. They taught me to dance. The coins must have jumped out of my pocket."

"Jumped out of your pocket! A likely story. How could this have happened?"

"Quite easily," the servant said. "You just put one foot here, touch the other toe there, and turn like this."

Soon the master and third servant were leaping and spinning in frenzied circles.

"It is now the master who is a fool," the first and second servants said to each other.

The master waved them off and continued dancing with the third.

# 44

The first voice was that of one of the students sitting among them. "This is an insult!" he cried. "You have brought God down to the level of a servant. How could such a lowly God also be king of the universe?"

When Jesus saw that the listeners were in agreement with the student, he told this story:

The angels asked the creator, "Why did you create Adam and Eve knowing they would err?"

"I did not create them to err; I planted the seed of freedom in them," the creator said, "thus I could not know what they would do."

"Why would you knowingly limit your knowing?" the angels replied.

"Because I wanted a creation in which you learn the most from those below you."

There were many questions. "Is there no divine wisdom?" "What can the ants teach us?" "How can we be guided by a God who follows us?" "Ha! Are we to walk in the path of snails?" "What do we know that we could teach the most high?"

"Quiet, quiet," said the rabbi. "Since our guest is a master of tales, I want to tell him a story of my own."

The rabbi told this story:

A student came to his teacher and declared that he had found the truth.

"Yes?" the teacher asked. "What is it?"

When the student told him, the teacher nodded and said, "You have found much that is true, but at least a tenth of the truth remains."

The student returned to his search. Years later he appeared before his teacher to report the result.

The teacher praised him. "You have all but a tenth of the remainder."

The next time the student appeared he was starved and penniless.

Again the teacher commended him. "Only a tenth of that fragment is yet to be found," he added.

The student returned to the quest but died before he found that last small piece.

The rabbi turned to Jesus. "If you tell one more story, your listeners will die of starvation and I will be deprived of the honor of serving you."

# 45

The light of morning was showing in the windows of the house of study before the discussion ended. As the people walked away to their own homes, two young men, wearing students' cloaks, caught up with Jesus who was following the rabbi to his home. Jesus saw that one of them was the student who thought he had insulted the king of the universe.

"My name is Thaddeus," this one said, speaking in Greek. "I have another question."

Jesus, fatigue showing in his face, did not reply.

"The priests teach that after death we are but lifeless dust," Thaddeus began. "The Pharisees teach that we are raised a new being. What is your teaching? Where does the soul go after we die?"

"I will answer that question," Jesus said, "when you tell me where the soul goes before we die."

Another student stepped forward. "I also have a question. It is written that life comes from dust and also returns to dust. Is there nothing more?"

"How much more could we ask for," Jesus replied, "than that dust turn to life?"

"Does the dust return to become life again in the next world?"

"Do our words become air when they die?"

The student hesitated for a moment. "Yes."

"Have you heard the air speak?"

Jesus turned and walked on. The first student reached out and took him by the sleeve. "Tell me this—if a man ascends into heaven and finds the throne of the most high empty, what would you tell him?"

"I would recite torah to him with the voice of a mule."

"The voice of a mule? Show me a mule that can talk."

"Show me a man who has ascended into heaven."

When the students went on to other questions, the rabbi waved them off and led Jesus into his house.

Later, when the students were asked what Jesus had said, they reported that he had told them the throne of God is empty.

# 46

The next day, as Jesus sat with his friends, the daughter of a prosperous coppersmith stood at a distance and listened to their conversation. When his friends had drifted away, she approached him.

"How can you have such followers," she asked him, "all of them plain, stupid, worthless?"

"In what kind of container," Jesus asked her, "does your father keep his olive oil?"

"In earthen jars."

"What? Not in gold and silver, and such a prosperous man?"

Later she asked her father why he did not keep his olive oil in gold and silver.

"I buy only the most precious oil," he said. "Gold and silver would ruin its taste. Why do you ask me this?"

The girl told him what Jesus had said.

Later that day the coppersmith met Jesus in the market where he was sitting with the Samaritan.

"Did you ask my daughter why her father does not keep his olive oil in gold and silver containers?"

Jesus nodded.

"I understand the meaning of this question," the coppersmith continued. "But I ask you, isn't it true that the rich and handsome can also be learned?"

"Yes, it is true. But if they were to become poor, ugly, and worthless their wisdom would increase manyfold."


# 47


It was nearly dark when a young man came to Jesus as he walked along the stony shore of the lake.

"I am Thaddeus, the one you mocked," the young man said with a faltering voice, "when I asked you about death."

"Why do you ask these questions about death, Thaddeus?"

"My mother and father . . . "

"Both dead?"

"When I was a child. My sister drowned . . . not far from here. And my brother . . . "

"You are alone."

"There is no one."

They walked together a way, neither of them speaking. The windless air was cool. Stars reflected off the surface of the lake. Jesus paused for a while then told Thaddeus this story:

A righteous man lived until his one hundred and thirtieth year. When the angel of darkness came to him, he placed a dazzling pearl in the old man's hand.

"Why do you give me this?" he asked. "The angel of darkness only takes away."

"I am grateful you let me catch up with you."

"Since it is too late for me to spend it," the old man thought, "I will leave it to my three sons."

The sons soon buried their father with all the honor due one so righteous. Quickly, however, they began to quarrel over the division of their inheritance.

One day a stranger appeared. He said he could divide the pearl in a way that would vastly increase the value of each portion. For the first time the brothers agreed and accepted the offer.

The stranger gently balanced the pearl on a flat rock then slammed another rock against it, grinding the pearl to a fine dust. He blew the dust into the air around the brothers, politely bowed, and walked away.

When they saw they shared nothing now but their poverty, they sorrowfully reconciled themselves. Only at the end of their long lives did they realize who the stranger was.


"How does this story answer my question?" Thaddeus asked.

"There is no answer to your question," Jesus said, "but get to know this stranger."

# 48

The next day Thaddeus came to Jesus with two of his fellow students. "I told them I talked with you and they asked why I called you 'rabbi.'"

"How could a rabbi," one of them asked, "say the throne of God is empty?"

"Nothing at all can be said with certainty," Jesus answered, "about the throne of God."

"But it is written that Isaiah himself saw God sitting on his high throne, his divine robe filling the temple."

"If torah says this, why did you ask me?"

"What you say diminishes torah."

"Whatever is said in response to torah only adds to it."

"Who could have knowledge great enough to add to it? Was it for nothing that God commanded us not to eat of the tree of knowledge?"

"Does God place ignorance above knowledge?"

When the students looked at each other, unsure how to answer this question, Jesus told this story:

God planted a garden and filled it with so many plants and animals that it took up the entire earth. Pleased with his work, he strolled its shaded forests, admired its gleaming beaches, and lay on the blowing prairies.

In time he found himself itching with an unexpected desire. He longed for something familiar in this endless abundance of growing things. He wanted to see his own image in the soul of another being.

It was difficult to create such a being, but when he had done so, he was alarmed to find that his restlessness was not calmed by the presence of this creature in the garden, for the creature had been infected by the very longing God meant to satisfy. So he divided this creature into two halves that imaged one another, one male and the other female.

Remarkably, this solution only made matters worse, for in addition to everything else they longed for each other. God perceived in the presence of the two a danger, though a danger sensed by none of the other creatures.

"They must be given limits," God said to himself. "They alone of all the plants and animals in the garden must be deprived of some part of their freedom."

"You may go anywhere," he said to them, "and do anything you wish. But one thing you may not do is eat of the tree of knowing."

Because of the fruitfulness of the garden the man and the woman thought this a harmless restriction. In time, however, they found themselves itching with a new desire. The woman especially longed for something she could find neither in this abundance nor in the man. She appealed to her fellow creatures.

"It is because of the tree of knowing," an emu told her.

"God made you in his image," said an iris, "then refused to let you live by it."

"To eat of that tree," explained an urchin, "is to become the equal of God."

"But why that tree?" the woman wondered.

"He wanted to protect you from knowing," said a whimbrel, "for every knowledge will give birth to an ignorance larger than itself, that ignorance to another knowledge and a still larger ignorance—thus to a desire as limitless as God's."

The woman doubted none of this wisdom but it only added to her nameless yearning. So early one morning, pulling the man behind her, she made her way to the forbidden tree.

The fruit had a distinctive sweetness. As she shared it with the man she said to herself, "It cannot be because of its taste that it is forbidden." She reached for more, and still more. Both of them, the man especially, found the more they ate, the more their appetite for it increased.

"Look," the woman cried. "Now we know why it is forbidden." She was pointing through the leaves at another figure raking fruit from the tree.

The three of them—the man, the woman, and God—looked at each other and knew, all three of them, what the others knew.

The students listened to the story in scornful silence. "Of course, it is merely fanciful," they said to themselves. "And its meaning is unclear." But later they often told it to others.

# 49

The next morning, after Jesus and his friends left the town of Capernaum and walked the road that followed the lake to the north, they overtook a gaunt wanderer. He stopped and asked each of their names, listening carefully to each.

"Why do you want to know our names?" Martha asked.

He pulled a sealed scroll from his cloak. "I am a messenger," he said. "I was sent by my master to find this person." He showed them what was written above the seal. It was a name partly worn away by the hand of the messenger.

"Why can't you return to your master and report that the person cannot be found?"

The messenger sighed. "I heard a rumor that my master has died. If so, his message may be even more important."

He sat at the side of the road and when the friends saw that he no longer listened to their suggestions, they resumed their journey.

Later Jesus said, "Those who speak only for another and not for themselves are bound to be lost."

# 50

As Jesus and his friends continued walking north away from Capernaum they were followed by some of those they had met there, among them Thaddeus, the coppersmith and his daughter, and a woman who said she was a seeress and called herself by the Latin name Eustacia.

An elegantly dressed young man who had been especially attentive at the house of study followed at a distance. He was accompanied by two slaves.

They stopped to watch fishermen pull in their catch from the night's fishing. When Jesus saw that the nets were heavy, he waded into the water and seized hold of a line. Several others joined in the labor. When the fish were laid out in the sun, the fishermen paused to eat and nodded to the others to join them.

The fishermen cut green sticks to hold the fish over the fire.

As they were eating, the coppersmith came next to Jesus.

"I heard the story you told about Adam and Eve and God in the garden. This can only be a false understanding of God."

"Is there only one understanding of God?" Jesus responded. "Or are there many?"

"Well, many."

"To each understanding aren't all the others false?"

The coppersmith thought about this. "But God must be perfect."

One of the fishermen had stopped eating and was listening closely to what Jesus and the coppersmith were saying.

"Do you seek perfection only for your God," Jesus asked, "or for yourself as well?"

"For myself as well. Yes."

"Beware of the faith that seeks perfection. It will draw you to a God who worships you more than you worship it."

"What shall I do then?"

"Be imperfect as your God is imperfect."

# 51

When Jesus and the coppersmith fell silent, the fisherman, whose name was Shimon, addressed both of them. "You speak of God. And you, too. So do many others. Who is the God you speak of? Does this God have a name like those of the Egyptians and the Greeks?"

Jesus blew the dried fish scales from his hands and told this story:

When Moshe descended with the law, the people were more interested in who gave it to him than what it commanded them to do.

"What does this God look like?" they wanted to know.

"It is a formless form and cannot be described," Moshe replied.

"Tell us the name of this God," the people demanded, "so we know whom to worship."

"The name is unspeakable," Moshe said. "It is a wordless name."

"Tell us," they begged. "Tell us!"

Moshe stepped back from them, then cried out the wordless name in a loud voice. The people fell down in awe when they heard it. Such was their amazement that some refused to believe in any being that would be called a name like this.

Those who believed spoke the name to each other, but quietly, for they feared they would create more unbelief. Each generation spoke the name more quietly until it became a silent name and was forgotten.

"I cannot speak the name of God," Jesus said, "because we have forgotten it."

Shimon seemed puzzled. "Why would a God allow his name to be forgotten?"

"It is our forgetting the name of God," Jesus said, "that makes peace among us possible."

## 52

Leaving the fishermen they made their way up into the hills above the lake, but slowly, for Nathanael's legs had become weaker.

After several days they came to a decaying Greek temple dedicated to Poseidon and paused to rest in its shadow.

"Havah, look at this," Jesus called to the child.

"What do you see?" she asked, crouching next to him.

"Look how fast the snail is moving."

"The snail isn't fast!" she said. "The ants are much faster."

"Do the ants then think they are better than the snail?"

"Oh, yes."

"What do you think they are saying to the snail?"

"What are they saying to the snail? The ants are saying, 'We have run many leagues today. We have seen much of the world. But you! You have only gone a few steps, looking always at the earth.'"

"How about the snail? Does it think itself better than the ants?"

"Oh, yes."

"What does it say to the ants?"

"What does it say to the ants? It says, 'You run back and forth over all the world but you never stop to see the riches that are beneath your feet.'"

"Do the snail and the ant listen to each other?"

"Oh, no."

"Should they?"

"They would learn so much if they did."

"So the snail's wisdom," said Jesus, "lies in the ants' experience and the ants' wisdom can be found in what the snail experiences, but neither knows it?"

"I suppose so."

# 53

A statue of Poseidon, the facial features worn away by the elements, looked west and south over the Lake of Galilee.

The seeress Eustacia stood before Poseidon. She opened her mouth and raised her arms, imitating the statue's pose. Then she started a slow dance around it as though the God had come to life.

"Ha!" said the grits dealer, Moshe. "Do you dare to mock the God?"

"Mock Poseidon?" Eustacia replied. "No. He is God of all those who live upon the sea and all those who have the sea within them."

"Then you mock the God of Israel," said Devorah.

"I mock none of the Gods," Eustacia said as she continued her flowing dance. "We need them all."

"We need none of them," said Judas in a firm voice.

"Not so!" Moshe declared and turned to where Jesus was sitting with Havah and the Samaritan. "You have a God," he called to him, "and is yours not the God of Israel?"

Jesus remained silent for a moment. "I have no God of my own," he said.

"That cannot be. Everyone has a God."

"Any God you have must exclude others, or you wouldn't call that God your own."

"I have a God because I am beset by others. I am the one who is excluded."

"Then you make your enemies the enemies of your God. This is a deadly division."

"It is not as you say," the grits dealer said. "The God of Israel protects us from our enemies in the world."

"The God of Abraham," Jesus said, "promised him he would be the father of a great people, but when Abraham died he had only two sons, one a deceiver, the other a bastard. The God of Moshe promised him a land but left him nothing. The God of David gave him a kingdom but let it slip away. Be careful how you use your Gods."

"How could we have a God who would not profit us?"

Jesus reclined against the feet of Poseidon and told this story:

A cedar took root at the edge of the bramble. Seeing how all beings were turned away from the bramble, the cedar said to it,

"Be my shield, for I am small, and unlike you I cannot protect myself."

The bramble said, "If I were your shield, I would be of no use to those who cut me each year to make a fence for their animals."

The cedar saw this was true. Whenever the bramble grew thick and strong, it was cut for fencing.

In time the cedar could see beyond the bramble where a field of wheat was blowing green in the sun. As the season passed it became a radiant gold. "Be my crown, for unlike you I have no gold of my own," the cedar begged the wheat.

"If I were your crown, I would be of no use to those who cut me each year for bread."

It was true. At the end of each season the ripe wheat was cut and carried from the field.

Beyond this field the cedar could now see a vineyard. "Be my fruitfulness," the cedar said to the vines, "for unlike you I bear nothing others desire."

"If we were your fruitfulness, what would those do who use my harvest each year for the wines that make so many glad?"

It was as the vine said. The cedar saw how each autumn gleeful harvesters cut the grapes and carried them to the winery.

Beyond the vineyard an orchard came into view. "Be my companions," the cedar said to the fig trees, "for unlike you I stand here alone."

"If we were your companions," the trees said, "we could be of no use to those who each year collect our fruit for their sweetness."

"But to whom can I be useful?" the cedar asked the trees, the vines, the wheat, and the bramble. "Does no one desire the fine wood I could provide them?"

"No one," they replied, "for while they were looking else-where you grew too tall and beautiful to be cut down. You are like a God become visible."

It was exactly as they said. Wherever the cedar looked, there were people who had stopped to gaze up at it in awe.

"But unlike you I cannot give them a shield and a crown, I cannot make them glad or give them fruit, or take their loneli-ness from them. There is nothing about me that profits them."

"It is because you profit no one," they said, "that you become a God for all those who behold you."

# 54

After they had slept and the sun had begun to set over the hill behind them, Devorah came to Jesus with Zakkai and Didymos and said, "In the days since the seeress came with us, each of us has seen an omen. We went to her to learn their meaning."

"What omens?"

"I saw an eagle drop a serpent onto a rock," Zakkai said, "where it was later eaten by a vulture."

"I opened an onion," said Devorah, "and found a stone in it."

"I opened a door to enter the house of one recently dead," said Didymos, "and the door came off its hinges."

"What did the seeress say to these omens?" Jesus asked.

"That I would profit from the errors of the powerful," said Zakkai.

"Though my life be frail and subject to rot," Devorah added, "it contains something both indestructible and unchanging."

"And you, Didymos?"

"What remains closed to me also shields me from death."

"Why are you telling me this?" Jesus asked.

"Should we listen to the seeress?"

"Look," Jesus said, pointing to an ant racing up his sleeve. It hesitated at a patched tear, ran down the same path, and dropped onto the dust. "An omen," Jesus declared.

"Why is this an omen?"

"What is not an omen?"

# 55

They walked south until they reached the edge of the lake. Passing through several small villages, they drew the attention of those standing about. Some of these idlers followed, making a small crowd of the curious.

The rich young man who had followed them from Capernaum, but always at a distance, approached Jesus and gestured to get his attention. "What is it you seek?" Jesus asked him when he saw the hesitation in the young man's face.

"I have followed you for some time now," he said in an

uneven voice. "I have listened to your words and closely observed your ways." He took a full breath and pulled at the neck of his tunic. "I now see that I have lived my life in vain."

"If you can see this," Jesus said to him, "then you have not lived your life in vain."

"I have thought about it deeply and wish to be one of your followers," the young man declared. Then pointing to his slaves who stood at the side, he said, "I will free my bonded servants, if you require it, and give all that I have to the poor."

"Your wealth is of no importance. Follow me by practicing your vanity boldly," Jesus replied. "Hide your vanity from others as you wish, but never hide it from yourself."

The young man hesitated. "That's all?"

"Nothing else is necessary."

He remained standing in the road as Jesus and the others continued.


# 56

Shortly after this, some of those who overheard this exchange came to Jesus.

Martha seemed the most puzzled. "Why did you not commend the young man," she asked, "for freeing his slaves and giving away all that he owns?"

"Why would I commend him for doing what he should do anyway?"

"But he was willing to take up a life of poverty," Zakkai said. "Is that not a merit?"

"Don't seek poverty by reducing your worldly possessions," Jesus said.

When they seemed not to understand, Jesus said, "The young man thought of poverty as a form of wealth. This could only increase his vanity."

"Is not poverty to be preferred over wealth?"

"Those who believe they are poor in worldly terms will soon be greedy in spiritual terms. Choose poverty for yourself. Protect others from it."

57

When they paused to wait for Nathanael, Didymos sat next to Jesus. "Perhaps it is true what is said, that the poor are always among us; we are poor ourselves, but must there always be those who cause the poverty of others for no reason but their own greed?"

"Yes."

"How can we make sense of a God who would permit such suffering?"

Jesus told this story:

Cain and Abel were equally skilled at planting and harvesting their fields. Each took pleasure in his own work and in his brother's.

One year Cain's harvest far outweighed Abel's. When Abel saw this, the pain of jealousy entered his heart and he requested that Cain share his surplus. But Cain, whose heart was filled with pride, refused. They quarreled. Abel struck him. In the ensuing fight Cain killed his brother.

When God came to him, Cain was standing in grief over Abel's fallen body.

"Why did you do this?" God asked him, pointing to the body.

"Why did you do *this*?" Cain answered, pointing to his heart.


"What did God answer?" Didymos asked.

"It is not God's question to answer."

"Whose then? Cain's?"

"Yours and mine."


# 58

Because of Nathanael they walked no further that day. After they had eaten they sat talking with each other until dark. A pale moon rose over the lake.

Following a long silence, Zakkai said to Jesus, "People ask us to tell them your message. We don't know what to answer.

We can tell them what you have said here or there, or we can tell them a story. But still they ask, 'What is he saying with all these words?' What shall we tell them?"

"Tell them what you yourselves have to say after what you have heard."

"How will we know that what we heard is what you have said?"

"What is heard is far more important than what is said."

When Jesus saw that Zakkai had still more questions, he told this story:

A messenger stopped a traveler on the road.

"This is for you," he announced breathlessly, handing the traveler a sealed scroll.

"How do you know this is for me?"

"Is this not your name?"

"Yes, but how do you know it?"

"I have looked for you a long time," the messenger answered.

The traveler noticed that the seal was stamped with the insignia of the king. "This is from the king?"

The messenger nodded. "Open it."

The traveler studied the document. There were only a few words. He was invited to appear before the king.

"I? I am to come before the king?"

"If that is what the message reads, yes," the messenger said. "But I am afraid that is now impossible, for the king has died."

"Why then have you delivered the message?"

"The king was living when he ordered me to bring this to you."

"You are obeying a dead king?"

The messenger shrugged. "It is a living invitation."

"It is a living invitation," the traveler said, "because you knew you could carry it out. What am I to do with a request I cannot obey even if I desired to do so?"

The messenger said nothing.

"Nothing so wonderful has ever happened to me," the traveler said, "that a king has sought me out by name. But now . . . " He sighed and looked down at the rich parchment. "This is a great loss. You say the king has died but I feel that it is I who died."

The messenger stared at the traveler with a blank face.

"Wait," the traveler suddenly exclaimed. "Take a message from me."

"Yes?"

"Tell the king that because I cannot appear before him, he is ordered to appear before me."

"This is impossible."

"It is no more impossible than the command given me by the king."

"How will I find him?" the messenger asked, leaning back with a disdainful expression.

"I can wait."

"What if you die first?"

"Waiting, I am alive."

The messenger raised his eyebrows, smiled ironically, and walked away.

"I have never been so alive!" the traveler called after him.


Nothing more was said.

# 59

A few days later, as they walked toward the village of Beth-saida in the heat of midday, they heard voices calling to them from a distance. They waited for a small band of travelers to reach them.

The travelers paused for a moment to catch their breath. When their eyes fell on Jesus, they grew still. "We are looking for Jesus of Galilee," one of them said to Jesus. "Is it you?"

"I am Jesus of Galilee. What is it you seek?"

The travelers had the appearance of wandering visionaries. Long strands of matted hair fell across their faces. They had rubbed ashes into their wretched clothes as a disinfectant and draped themselves with strings of dried figs and locusts.

"Yohanan sent us," said the one who had spoken. He lifted a small earthen vial from his robe. "You are to be anointed."

Jesus held up his hand. "By what authority does Yohanan send you here?"

"Yohanan possesses no powers of his own. He told us authority belongs to you alone."

"But I will not be anointed."

"It is not Yohanan who does this. He knows from a vision that you are already anointed."

"Return this oil to Yohanan."

Jesus' friends had drawn close to hear what was being said. No one moved.

The visionary lifted the vial. "This is but an earthen symbol," he said, and threw it to the ground where it shattered. "It is God's power alone to anoint. It is not Yohanan but God who declares you the anointed one."

"Do you speak for God or for Yohanan?"

"To be in Yohanan's presence is to know he is filled with God."

"I trust only those," Jesus said, "who know they are empty of God."

The visionary straightened and looked down at Jesus. "It is Rome above all that is empty of God. For that reason God will begin by first cleansing the earth of this Godless people."

A butterfly danced between them. Jesus reached out to touch it and it circled away. "So Yohanan teaches that I am to begin this cleansing?"

"You are to do nothing. The work of God alone will bring the present age to an end. It is Yohanan's teaching that you are the first citizen of the coming age."

Jesus shrugged and turned away.

"It is also Yohanan's teaching that you will reject all that we told you. 'This is the first sign,' he said to us."

Jesus seemed not to hear these last words as he resumed his journey. His friends, troubled by what was said, begged Yohanan's disciples to explain his strange teaching. But they, satisfied with what they had done, turned and walked toward Jerusalem without another word.

# 60

Later some of the friends asked each other, "Can it be that he is the anointed one?"

Though they were full of wonder, no one dared answer. Then Levi said, "Yohanan speaks the truth but it's a truth neither he nor his followers understand."

They looked at the blind man but said nothing.

# 61

Not many days later they entered a village north of the Lake of Galilee and came to the house of one recently dead. Mourners were standing about quietly talking with each other.

"Who has died?" one of the friends asked.

"Our learned and saintly rabbi," they responded.

A student was standing to the side. His chest was heaving with grief.

"Why are you weeping?" Jesus asked him.

"I am not grieving for rabbi," the student answered. "No one knew more torah than rabbi. I can only think of the great knowledge he can no longer share with us."

"There were times," said another mourner, "when rabbi put so much effort into learning torah that he could not rise from his chair or carry his own cloak. After long periods of study he could not speak. We fed him with our own hands."

"How can I not weep?" added the student. "Think of the knowledge of torah known only to rabbi that died with him."

"Nothing died with him," Jesus said.

The mourners, offended, asked him, "Why do you say, 'Nothing died with him'?"

"What we have not taught to others," Jesus said to them, "is not knowledge."


# 62


When the student repeated this remark to some of the other guests, one of them, a rich old man, was amazed and asked, "Who said this to you?"

"That one, dressed like a beggar."

"Tell him," the old man said, "that he and his friends are welcome to come to my house this evening."

"Why would you ask someone like this?" the student protested. "And those with him? Surely you would not invite such low and unclean vagabonds to your table. One is blind, another leprous, another an idiot. And there are women as well."

"If you quoted him correctly, I can see that he has much to say to us. Go to him now. Tell him all are invited. Yes, even the—vagabonds. The women, too, are welcome."

When evening came and they had gathered in the old man's large house, he greeted Jesus and his friends as honored guests.

When he had placed bread and olives before them, he turned to Jesus and, with amusement in his eyes, asked, "Did you say, 'What is not taught to others is not knowledge'?"

"I said this. And is it not true?"

"Do you also say that torah is not torah until it is taught?"

"How could it be any different?"

"There is no torah until it is taught?"

Jesus brushed away a flying insect. "Until it is taught there is nothing but ink on parchment."

The old man smiled at this remark. "So then whatever is taught as torah is torah?"

"For that reason teaching can be done only with great care."

"But each word was given Moshe by God. Does it not then have the meaning God gave it?"

"Each word has a meaning not even God could comprehend."

"How could this saying be anything but blasphemy?"

Jesus spit an olive seed into his hand. "Do you know what will come of this seed? Will it become a tree? Will it be beautiful? Deformed? Will it supply the tables of the wicked? Will it live through a dozen empires?"

"Where do you find teaching such as this in torah?"

"If you wish to know whether I understand torah, why do you ask me to quote it?" he asked the old man and told this story:

A pious merchant one day opened his door to an ill-dressed man.

"I know you share your great learning with others," the man said. "Would you also share the abundance of your table with a beggar?"

"Only if you could answer certain simple questions of torah."

When the beggar could not open his mouth on the subject, the merchant turned him away.

Later a friend asked why he refused the man. When the merchant told him, the friend said, "Don't you know this beggar is more learned in torah than all of us?"

"Then why did he not answer my questions?"

"Because he did not want to insult scripture by profiting from his knowledge of it."

The old man laughed. "So torah is not the end but the beginning of knowledge?"

"At least that."

"So the end of knowledge cannot be knowledge itself?"

Jesus nodded.

The old man thought for a moment. "There was a saintly scholar named Elihu, of blessed memory, who lived here many years ago, when I was still a boy. There are many tales about him. It is said that when the angel of death came he refused to go with him but placed his staff on the ground and leapt straight into paradise. He taught us much but most of all he taught us to be modest in our learning. He once told us this story":

When a certain rabbi of great knowledge arrived in paradise, the Most High came at once to meet him. "My friend," God said to him, "you are famed here for your learning but do you know all my teachings on creation?"

When the rabbi had correctly recited the teachings on creation, God indicated his approval.

"Do you know my teachings on the exodus?"

After the rabbi had answered this question at length, he was
questioned on the kings and prophets of Israel, and the psalms.
Pleased to display his learning to the source of it, the scholar
declared, "I have learned all that you have taught. Isn't that
why I am here?"

"It is true that you know all that I have taught," the Most
High responded. "But you don't know me. It is for that reason
that you are here."

# 63

Soon they reclined for supper and others entered the discussion of these matters.

While they were eating, one of the Pharisees said to Jesus,
"Let me test you on the law." He looked about at those who had
come with Jesus. "Everywhere you go there are women with
you. I have watched carefully the way you are with the men
and the women. You are with one as you are with the other.
Where in torah is this required?"

"Where is it forbidden?"

"Is it not written that Eve is made of an inferior part of Adam's flesh?"

"It is written that God put Adam to sleep then created Eve. What is Eve therefore but Adam's awakening? If there were no Eve, Adam would still sleep. We would be but Adam's dream."

A second Pharisee raised his voice. "I am angered by your use of torah. I, too, want to test you on the law."

"If the words of torah were received with fire," Jesus said, "how can we talk about them except with fire?"

The Pharisee placed two pickled locusts on his open hand. "If one of these is consecrated and the other is not consecrated but they are packed into the same jar and you don't know which is clean and which is unclean, is it unclean to eat them?"

"According to the law, yes, certainly," Jesus said.

"What if I told you, falsely, that they are both consecrated? Have you still done something unclean?"

Jesus hesitated. "No. Not if I didn't know."

"So it is your awareness that determines whether your life is unclean?"

"Yes."

A soft breeze came through the open windows where several listeners had gathered. The single flame of the oil lamp flickered and went out. No one rose to relight it.

"You are aware," the second Pharisee said, "that the rich steal from the poor. You are aware that the priests are false teachers of torah. You are aware that Rome rules us with injustice and cruelty. Does your awareness of these make you unclean?"

"If I do nothing about it," Jesus said, "I am unclean."

"Is your awareness higher than the law? For there is no law that requires you to do something in this case."

There was a silence in the darkened room. No one moved.

"It is the nature of the law," Jesus said, "to go beyond itself."

"How can the law go beyond itself? It is the law of God after all."

Someone brought in a coal from the fire and lighted the small lamp.

"We do not become righteous by faithfully obeying each of the 613 laws in the torah."

The Pharisee turned out his hands in a gesture of impatience and left the house.

# 64

The old man who first questioned Jesus shook his head slowly and said, "You place a great obstacle before the student of torah. For the simple it is difficult enough to understand even a few of the laws. No one is so learned as to understand them all. Now to go beyond them . . ."

"Before torah we all are simple," Jesus said.

"This is certainly not true," the old man responded. "Aren't some wiser than others?"

Jesus pondered the question for a moment then told this story:

All the people of the earth came together in one great city, desiring to speak one tongue and to make a single nation out of many. They raised grand buildings, shared their wealth, and appointed fair judges to resolve all conflicts.

But when they had done these things, an unease came over them. The poets went silent. The heroes grew old and were forgotten. There was no singing and laughter was rare.

"We have finished building our city but it is incomplete," said one of the sages. The others agreed but no one could say what needed still to be done.

One day God was seen strolling through the streets gazing up at the towers and spires. The sages came in a run and were soon telling God the history of their triumph. "But there is something missing," they admitted. "Just what we don't know."

"It is true. You have perfected human speech," God said. "But what you lack is the perfection of divine speech."

At once the sages asked for the gift of divine speech.

God touched each of them on the lips. Each began to speak a tongue unknown to the others. When every citizen had been touched, the city became a roar of incomprehension.

The people wandered off in all directions hoping to find a place where they could be understood. Slowly the city decayed. The buildings fell into themselves and turned to dust. Then it was forgotten. So was its perfected human speech.

"What is the meaning of this story?" the old man asked. The others were silent, waiting for Jesus' explanation.

"Until we can speak all the tongues the people of the earth speak," he said, "we will be too simple to understand divine speech."

# 65

In the morning, as Jesus was awakened by his host, the old man announced to him that a crowd of villagers was waiting for him at the door. "Hearing you are called 'rabbi,' they have brought their sick to be healed. What shall I tell them?"

"Wake my friends. I will leave by the back door with those who will go with me."

The old man waited.

"Tell them I have no such powers."

By late morning they had found their way back to the lake. Judas was walking at the side of Jesus and the Samaritan woman. Jesus was holding the hand of Bartholomew who now and then burst into hysterical laughter at nothing in particular.

"Your torah," Judas said, speaking with his philosopher's voice. "It provokes questions. I heard what you said about divine speech, but isn't it the other way around? Aren't the words of your torah too simple to have a clear meaning?"

Hatches of fleas rose from their footsteps on the graveled beach then drifted off on the wind.

"How the world begins, for example," Judas continued. "Man and woman in the garden. You have retold the story very differently from your torah. I, too, can make this child's tale say many things. Exactly what is its meaning?"

The nets of fisherman, hung out on racks, rose and fell on the wind. A few small dried fish flashed in the sun. Jesus picked them off, ate several whole, and gave one to Bartholomew. When Jesus saw that Bartholomew put it in his ear, he told this story:

The God of the garden told Adam and Eve there was one tree from which they must take nothing, lest they be poisoned by it and forced to leave the garden. Later Eve asked Adam if he knew why this tree was a danger to them.

"It is no different from the others," she said.

Adam didn't know. Nor did it matter to him.

She asked the same question of their animal companions. None could answer it. Neither did it matter to them. In time, it was all that mattered to Eve. Then she asked the serpent.

"This tree," the serpent said, "hides a treasure most rare. But it is a treasure only to you. For the God of the garden it is a poison he fears above all other things. He said you cannot possess it and remain in the garden. He lied. The truth is that if you were to possess it he could not remain God of the garden."

"What then is it?" Eve asked the serpent.

"You can only know by making it yours."

Eve looked up at the tree.

"Shake it," the serpent said.

Eve shook it. A strange sound came from all parts of the tree. She stepped back. "What is this?"

"Laughter."

"What can I do with it?"

The serpent said nothing, only laughed. Then Eve laughed. Soon Adam heard them and he, too, laughed.

Later in the day the God of the garden caught them playing with each other. "What are you wearing?" he asked, seeing that they had draped one another with banana and palm leaves.

"Adam dresses as I want," Eve said, "and I dress as Adam wants."

Judas stood in the path and waited.

"This," Jesus said, "is how the world begins."

# 66

Judas said nothing more but that evening he reported this conversation to Levi. "He only gave the meaning of one child's story by telling another."

"Why should there be but one meaning?" Levi asked.

"There are others? Is there no end to this . . . storytelling?"

"Judas, you are a master of speech," Levi said. "Become a master of silence as well. Know when words that do not cease cease being words."

# 67

Late in the day, they entered a small fishing village where they hoped to find food. But the village seemed abandoned; no one was in sight. Soon they understood why.

Standing in the center of the village was a troop of soldiers.

They were drinking from flasks of wine they had taken from the villagers.

As Jesus and his friends appeared, the soldiers halted their revelry. When they saw there were cripples and children among the friends, and also women and an idiot and a blind man, their faces lighted with dangerous smiles and they started toward them with uneven steps.

The friends backed up as far as they could for they knew what drunken soldiers were likely to do with them. Then they saw that Jesus was walking straight through the small square, close to the soldiers, looking at the ground as he often did, oblivious to what was around him.

One of the soldiers pushed him at the shoulder, spinning him in their direction. Jesus stopped and looked at the faces of each of them as they gathered in a semicircle several arm lengths away, one pushing the other to start their cruel games. But no one stepped closer.

Jesus waited but said nothing. Then he continued through the square, looking at the ground as before. His friends followed.

The next day, still amazed, they talked with each other about what had happened. "What is this strange power he has," Nathanael asked, "that he can make armed and drunken soldiers back off without raising a hand?" The others had the same question. They became convinced this is a divine gift, that he possesses greater powers than a mere human could have.

"He has no power at all," Levi said. "The soldiers stepped away because they saw in his face that he could not be shamed."

The friends were certain Levi was wrong. Still, they wondered how a blind man could see the face of Jesus.

# 68

Several days later, Didymos, remembering what Jesus had said at dinner in the house of the old man, asked him, "Why did you say we cannot become righteous by obeying all 613 laws? What else should we obey?"

Jesus told him this story:

Solomon, knowing in his wisdom how easily the law can be forgotten, summoned thirty scholars to his palace. He fed and housed them until each had memorized all 613 of the laws.

When they had completed the task, a divine voice announced that there was one more law given to Moses but forgotten in ancient times. The scholars clamored to learn it.

"I will tell it only to the youngest in your company," the voice answered.

They looked about. They were chagrined to find the youngest among them was a servant girl. "Withdraw from her," said the voice, "and I will teach her."

The astonished scholars withdrew.

Later the girl told them the voice commanded her to keep secret what was told her until the time of her death. She lived a long and unexceptional life. When the time of her death drew near, the surviving scholars gathered around her. She struggled to speak. The scholars leaned close to hear.

"I forgot it years ago," she said with her last breath.

"Forgot it!" Didymos protested. "If that were so, it would be impossible to lead a perfectly righteous life."

"Yes," Jesus said.

# 69

Fishermen hailed Jesus from their boat. When they saw that Jesus could not hear them above the sound of the wind and waves, one of them sprang into the water and swam ashore. It was Shimon.

"I have longed to see you again," he said when he had got his breath. "We have heard many speak of your powers. We have often told the story we heard from you. Few understand it but they want themselves to hear your words."

Amri pulled the boat onto the sand and stood with Shimon. They begged Jesus to visit their small village on the other side of the Lake of Galilee. Jesus shook his head.

"Ten years ago," Shimon explained, "Onias the wonder-worker came to us and performed many miracles. The people were amazed and some followed Onias. But soon the sick who had been healed were sick again and the crippled took up crutches they had thrown away."

"You think I'm a prophet that I can perform such wonders?" Jesus answered.

"We no longer look to wonderworkers," Shimon said. "Another kind of healing is needed. The people have suffered greatly under Rome and they hunger for justice."

"Achieving power over Rome," Jesus said, "is this the wonder they expect me to perform?"

"They expect only that you will come and talk with them. Come."

Jesus went with him.

# 70

Many joined them. They set off in several boats.

They were the Samaritan woman with Jesus; a rice merchant named Mavgai; the widow Devorah; Levi; Joram; Bartholomew with Zakkai; Didymos; Martha; an old man called Nicodemus who had lost his hearing and often his memory; the student Thaddeus; Yaakov the leper; Shimon with his brother Amri; the coppersmith with his daughter; Nathanael with Havah; and the seeress Eustacia, who hesitated but came aboard at the last moment.

Before they departed, Judas bid Jesus a hasty farewell, announcing he must travel to Jerusalem. "I am summoned," he said, "to speak with the governor, Pilatus. If good fortune is mine, I will find you on the road once more."

As they took their places in the boats, others watched but did not join them.

"There are too many of us," Zakkai warned, looking at the seeress with suspicion.

"The wind is high but the sea is calm," said Shimon.

Jesus seated himself on the bottom, his back to the bow.

Shortly before reaching the shore the wind rose sharply. The oarsmen saw white lips of foam on the waves and pulled harder. The gale struck with such fury it muted the cries of terror. Water poured over the sides of the boat.

"Only a miracle could save us," someone called out. They turned to Jesus and found that he was asleep, his head on the shoulder of the Samaritan. A half-dozen hands reached out to wake him.

He woke slowly and looked up at them.

"Save us!" several of them cried.

"What? Do you think I can command the wind and the waves?" he asked, rebuking them. "Live by the storm or die by it. There is nothing else."

Soon the fishermen had the boats under control and minutes later were pulling them onto the beach. As the oarsmen handed the passengers over the gunwales, they shrugged with indifference at the expressions of relief. "We were never in danger," one of them boasted.

# 71

Shimon sent word ahead then led Jesus and the Samaritan up the rocky hill toward the village, now obscured by clouds of dust and straw raised by the wind. By the time they reached the small gathering of people waiting for them, a cold rain was blowing.

The villagers, about thirty in number, stood in small groups covering their faces against the weather. Jesus sat on the ground before them.

For a while none of them dared to speak. Then a young stonecutter, his rough cloak whitened with lime, stepped forward. He looked around at his fellow citizens, as though he had been assigned to speak for them.

"Each year," he began, "the Romans tighten their iron rule and demand a higher tax from us. Some say the occupation is what God has imposed on us. Is this what you say?"

"This," Jesus said, "is just what the Romans want us to believe."

"Others call for rebellion."

"This too is what the Romans want, for violence on one side justifies violence on all sides."

"What then?" said the young stonecutter, his voice rising with impatience. "Suffer in passive silence?"

Jesus looked at the ground before him, a troubled look on his face. After a pause, he said, "We are never excused from opposing bondage, whether of ourselves or of others."

The crowd pushed closer, trying to hear the words of the speakers over the wind.

"But this requires a power none of us has," the young stonecutter said. "Not even the armed insurrectionists can stand against Rome."

"Then it can only be that something greater than power is required," Jesus told him.

"What could be greater than power, if it is not more power?"

Jesus' answer was lost in the wind. The listeners turned to each other but none had understood.

The stonecutter spoke again, in a bolder voice. "We heard what you said to the Roman centurion at the entrance to Capernaum. You met the Roman's sword with words. Are these your weapons—words?"

"You see that I have no sword. And," he said looking about him, "you can see I have no army. You are right to question whether words are enough. Perhaps there is something greater even than words."

Jesus grew silent. The listeners came closer to hear how he might answer the stonecutter.

"Rome," Jesus said at last, "has its life nowhere but in our awe and fascination. Thus if we can be oblivious to Rome, Rome cannot touch us."

"What? Oblivious to Rome when it tyrannizes us?"

"Rome will not die until it dies in our hearts."

The young man hesitated, not certain he heard these words correctly.

Another came forward. "Armed insurrection alone is what needs now to be planted," he declared. "Even if it leads to martyrdom."

"Avoid martyrdom," Jesus said. "What we buy for ourselves with martyrdom others will pay for with their lives."

"Still Rome is great and we are small."

"An ox is big enough to pull a tree from the ground," Jesus said, "but it is too big to plant one."

"What then are we to plant?" another villager called out, mocking Jesus. "Do we meet evil with love?"

Jesus did not answer at once but looked at the villager for a moment. "No," he said, "beware of love, for love is evil's fondest home. The antidote to evil is curiosity. We won't destroy what we desire to know."

"Rome is an empire under the rule of one man," said another. "But we have no Augustus. The people are not of one mind in opposing Rome. Many will stand in our way. How can we pull the thistles from the wheat?"

Jesus pointed at the hills around them. "You are about to plant your spring crops," he said. "Not one of you will go out to plant weeds, but no field is planted well enough that weeds won't grow among the grain. But treat the weeds with respect. There may be a cedar among them and we may not live long enough to know it. Weeds that outlive us are not weeds."

The people turned to each other. "What did he say?" No longer able to hear his words in the storm, the villagers returned to their homes. Jesus and his friends took what shelter they could among the rocks.

# 72

Nathanael led Levi to a shallow overhang and sat next to him. They remained there for a while, neither speaking. Finally Levi turned to Nathanael. "I can see that you are troubled."

"The people haven't heard what he says," Nathanael answered.

"If that troubles you," Levi responded, "then you haven't heard what he says."

# 73

The rain stopped during the night and the sky cleared. Just before the sun appeared, Jesus and the Samaritan rose from where they were sleeping and walked to the top of the hill.

When the light of the rising sun struck them, they held out their clothes to dry in the unexpected warmth of an early breeze.

Then they sat in silence as the morning gathered itself around them.

The Samaritan was the first to speak. "The young stone-cutter's question is also your question."

Jesus stood, turned his back to the sun, and looked down over the lake and the hills of Galilee beyond.

"Yes, words are necessary," she said. "But it is true as you say that there is something greater than words. Yes, Rome must die in us. But it is true that there is something greater even than that. Is it this 'greater' you have still to seek?"

"When I walked away from Jerusalem," Jesus said to her, "it was to leave all that was Rome behind us. But it is not possible to walk away from what is everywhere around us. And within us. Its false eternities have seduced us. Even the stonecutter. His thoughts of winning justice from Rome are the thoughts of a Roman."

"So in this Yohanan is wrong," the Samaritan said. "Rome is not empty of divinity."

"The Gods can live nowhere else."

The Samaritan's gaze followed Jesus as he paced the summit of the hill.

"The stonecutter," he said, "wants to be free of Rome. But there is something that comes before and is far more difficult—

to free Rome of the Gods. First by taking the measure of our own false worship."

She neither moved nor spoke.

"How to do this?" he asked himself, studying the horizon as it slowly backed into the haze of midday heat. "How can we know until the moment arrives? I know only that the moment will arrive for each of us. At least once."

"Come then," she said and started down the hill.

# 74

Among the others only Eustacia had been awake when Jesus and the Samaritan rose that morning and started up the hill.

She watched them as they made their way to the crest then stood looking east. When the first light reached them, they held up their cloaks to dry. The sun painted their bodies with gold and made shining flags of their clothes.

Eustacia sat up, pressed her hands against her eyes, and looked again. She gasped and fell back. Martha, lying next to her, woke and asked her what had happened.

Eustacia, unable to speak, pointed to the top of the hill. Martha looked but saw nothing.

"What is it?" she asked the seeress. "Was something there?"

"He was touched by the fire of heaven."

"Who?"

"Angels descended and took him up. Then everything turned dark."

"Did you hear anything?"

Eustacia thought for a moment. "There was a voice."

"What did it say?"

"'*Obey him.*' Only that. '*Obey him.*'"

Martha looked about. She saw that Jesus and the Samaritan were not there. "Tell no one of this," she said to Eustacia.


# 75


It was nearly midday before Jesus appeared. Without saying anything to the others, he helped Zakkai to his feet and began walking in a direction away from the village. The rest gathered their small belongings and followed.

Later that day Martha took Didymos aside and told him what had happened, urging him to tell no one else.

When Didymos was alone with Nathanael, he pledged him to secrecy then reported what he had heard. Nathanael entered into the same confidence with Zakkai and Shimon. Yaakov too was told but he spoke not a word about it. Soon it was a secret they all shared, all except Levi.

Over the next several days, the friends frequently spoke with each other about the meaning of Eustacia's strange vision, especially since she recalled more detail—flashes of light, other voices, Elijah descending and placing his hands on Jesus.

It was Devorah who was the first to say that they were in the presence of the messiah. "It is exactly what Yohanan sent his disciples to tell us. He is the anointed one. What else can this vision mean?"

When the others heard this they were doubtful, but as they talked among themselves, they too began to wonder, for they had not forgotten the strange message of Yohanan's followers.

Martha, however, was skeptical of Eustacia's account and suggested that they ask Jesus directly.

"He will not answer directly," Nathanael said, "for if he had wanted us to know he would have told us from the beginning."

"Then let us ask him indirectly," Thaddeus declared. The others agreed.

# 76

Later, when Thaddeus was walking alone with Jesus, he said, "You did not answer the young stonecutter when he asked how Rome will be destroyed. Do you believe this will happen?"

"Yes," Jesus answered.

"But who would do this?"

"Why does it matter?"

"Do you also believe there will be a messiah?"

Jesus hesitated before answering. "Yes."

"Where do you believe we will find him?"

"When you know how to look," Jesus said, "you could find the messiah anywhere."

"What would he look like?"

"This we will know only when the messiah appears."

"Would the messiah know who he was?"

Jesus seemed surprised by this question. "The messiah least of all."

"So he could be anyone?"

"Anyone. And anywhere."

"None of this is found in torah," Thaddeus said. Jesus did not respond. "Are we then to forget torah?"

"When we live torah so completely that it lives in us, then we will neither remember nor forget it. Our simplest words will be filled with holiness."

"For those who do this the messiah has come?"

When Jesus saw Thaddeus' perplexity, he told him this story:

A rich man announced a banquet, inviting the whole city, but he failed to indicate the time and place. Some thought the rich man was making a joke at their expense. Some thought he was simply mad. Others took the missing information as proof they had been excluded, that the banquet was only for those with a special knowledge of the rich man's private affairs.

Some, but only a few, went one by one to the rich man's house to ask him directly.

"When is this banquet? And where?"

"Now! Here!" he cried to each of them as they arrived and conducted them at once to a sumptuous dinner at his own table.

Thaddeus was silent for a moment. "Who is the rich man in this story? The messiah?"

"You are the rich man," Jesus said. "Each of us is a wealth for the others."

# 77

When Thaddeus reported this conversation to the others, some of them were even more convinced. "As I said," Nathanael declared, "he will not tell us directly."

"Look for signs of power," Shimon said. "If he is the messiah, he cannot long remain hidden."

"Why is it important to know?" Levi asked.

They were startled by the question.

"Because of Eustacia's vision," Shimon said.

"What vision?"

Didymos repeated the seeress's account in complete detail, then waited for Levi's response.

"The greater gift," Levi said, rocking gently where he sat, "is not to see what others don't see, but what they do see."

# 78

When they woke the following morning, Jesus was sitting at a distance with the Samaritan. The two were in solemn conversation and oblivious to the others.

"What does it mean that he removes himself like this?" Zakkai asked.

"It is often so," added Nathanael.

When Jesus returned, he prepared to resume their journey but said nothing about where they were going.

Later that day a man passed by with a cow and her newborn calf. He pulled the calf by a rope. Untethered, its mother walked quietly behind.

Noticing their curiosity, the man said, "I wanted to take the cow to the slaughterhouse but she resisted. This way, she comes."

Later Jesus said to his friends, "Beware of love. It can take you where you shouldn't go."

# 79

When night came they made a small charcoal fire, wrapped themselves in their cloaks, and gazed at the sky in silence.

Then Martha came to Jesus. "Two times you have spoken of love. Once that love can be a dwelling place for evil. And today that love can lead us where we shouldn't go. How can we live with each other without love?"

Jesus added a handful of sticks to the fire and blew on them until a flame appeared. "Love is not necessary," he said.

"Shouldn't we love those next to us?"

"You can live next to those you despise."

"Despise them and still live among them? How could we then be neighbors?"

"We are truly neighbors only when we know we can live together without loving each other."

"Then my neighbors can also be my enemies. How am I to understand this?"

"If they know that being a people together is greater than their hatred for each other, they can be neighbors."

"There is a teaching of the rabbis," Martha said, "that we should love our enemies."

"It is much less important to love our neighbors," Jesus responded, "than to understand that we, too, are enemies."

When Jesus saw that Martha was puzzled, he told her this story:

A king received a message from the ruler of a neighboring land. The royal translators hesitated to tell him what it said. The king demanded to know why.

"He has slighted you," the royal translators answered.

The king ordered them to recite the message in his own tongue. He was a cruel despot, the message said, deaf to the cries of widows and orphans. So driven by greed he starves his peasants and wrongly claims title to the lands of other kings. Moreover, he is a coward on the field of combat.

"Such insults cannot be endured," he announced to his court. "I have no choice but to declare war at once."

The enemy, prepared for this sudden turn, slyly abducted the king's young daughter and held her for ransom. Fearing for her life, the king withdrew his armies.

As the years passed the king, still furious at the insults and grieving the loss of his only child, carefully waited until the enemy thought the danger of war had passed. He arranged a surprise assault and his daughter, no longer a girl, was rescued.

To the king's dismay, he found she had forgotten her native tongue and now spoke only the words of the enemy. Unable to exchange a single word with her, he ordered the royal translators to teach him to think and speak in this strange language.

As this instruction progressed, the king spent hours listening to the princess's tales of her childhood in a foreign place. He grew increasingly jealous of his old enemy as the princess described the warmth of the ruler's family and especially his kindness to her.

"How can you say this?" he cried out one day in anger. "This man is a brutal master of his hungry people, covetous of his neighbors, a craven soldier!"

When the king understood that what he had said of the hated king was exactly what that enemy said of him, he stood and quickly left the princess.

Shortly afterward he surrendered the throne to her. She immediately brought peace to both kingdoms.

# 80

"Someone is passing by," said the blind man. "It is several people. Ten, perhaps fifteen."

Staring into the dark, they could make out movements in the field below them. It looked as though the rocks themselves were in motion. Then they saw that these were human figures walking in a line and soundlessly.

"It is against the law to change places after dark," said Joram. "They must be thieves."

The wanderers stopped. At a signal from one of them, they walked up to where the friends were lying.

Their leader, a tall and stern young man, stepped forward. "Do you have food?"

"Only some dried fish, a few citrons, and water," Zakkai replied.

"Feed these men what you have." He took only a little water while the others ate. Then he looked closely at each of those seated there. When he came to Jesus, he stopped. Jesus stared back at him. Neither spoke.

"We thought you were thieves," said Joram.

The leader dropped to his knees and held his hands over the last of the coals.

"We are at war with thieves," he said, "thieves who steal your food, your liberty, and, if you are not vigilant, your souls."

"But there is peace in Galilee, and peace in Palestine," said Thaddeus.

"There is peace only for those who want to be ruled by priests. But these are not priests. Even though they build palaces for themselves, they are slaves of Rome. Their greatest pleasure is in hating their own people."

"What do you plan to do," Shimon asked, "destroy Rome?"

"By first destroying the temple, stone by stone, priest by priest."

"It took many thousands of laborers and many years to put these stones in place," said Shimon. "There are so few of you and some of the stones are the size of houses. You think you will undo them with these . . . sticks?"

"The labor of destruction will be left to the Romans."

"What? Now you will have the Romans do what you cannot? What will make them do so?"

"They will do so only when they fear our people," the captain said.

"Your people? These?"

"True, we are few in number. But each of us will bring another to the struggle, and each of those another. In a day, a year, ten years—how long, it doesn't matter—we will be greater than Rome."

"And then?"

"We will drive them out of Judea. Then if necessary we will take Rome itself from them."

When no one spoke to this, Levi said to the commander, "You are brave with your arms. It is your thinking that lacks courage."

Ignoring Levi's remark, the commander looked into each face as he had before. "You," he said to Shimon, "come with us. You, too," he said to another. "And you." Then his eye fell on Levi. "But not you! How can we fight the blind with the blind?" Some of his followers laughed.

Then he looked long at Jesus but neither of them spoke.

Seeing that no one would come with him, he said, "You will pay for your cowardice. Those that aren't with us are against us."

He walked away. His ragged soldiers followed.

# 81

When they saw that the insurrectionists were gone, Nathanael turned to Jesus. "What sense is there in the words of this ruffian? If the temple already belongs to the Romans, why would they tear it down?"

Before Jesus could answer, the coppersmith said, "It is a teaching of the rabbis that the tyranny of Rome will end only when the walls of Jerusalem are pulled down by a righteous leader, a king who rises from the people, a messiah whose hand is guided by the hand of God."

Martha doubted this. "I have heard rabbis say that the messiah will come as a secret teacher leading the chosen to sanctuary in the wilderness."

"Where is the wilderness that can hide a whole people?" cried the coppersmith.

"Where is the army," answered Martha, "that will take Jerusalem from Rome?"

As the dispute continued, others entered with their own opinions.

"Like the baptizer," said one, "I see a divine messenger who comes on wings of fire to punish the unrighteous."

"I am with the insurrectionists," said another. "Only when we all rise with iron in our hands will Rome fall."

"You are all wrong," said Joram the scribe. "The chosen of God will not destroy Rome, they will not flee it, nor will God bring the earth to a terrible end. God has given us all that is necessary: torah. God will shelter those who study and live by divine law. There will be many empires after this one. We will live as peacefully in one as in another."

"How can it be," Martha asked, "that all these empires will allow us to live our lives as we wish?"

"If we do not despise Rome," Joram said, "why would Rome despise us?"

Jesus looked troubled but said nothing to this.

# 82

When they ceased talking, Shimon turned to Jesus. "You were silent while the partisans were here. Had you nothing to say to the leader of these violent men?"

"He spoke only the truth."

"You believe that these few hungry youths will pull down the temple?"

"Everything made to contain the holy makes its own destruction inevitable."

"He also said he would take Rome from the Romans. Where is the truth in that?"

Jesus stared at the fire between them. They waited for his answer. "Every Rome will fall but only at the hand of another Rome."

"How could one Rome follow another?"

"You heard the commander speak of 'our' people," Jesus replied. "He didn't speak of what this people might become but of what they already are and continue to be. His is a people that places itself outside time, an eternal Rome. Whatever people declares itself timeless is bound to be pushed aside by another."

"Are we not also a people?"

"Yes, but not Levi's people or Martha's or Shimon's."

"Can we be a people without a name?"

"With a name we soon become 'our' people to ourselves, 'their' people to others."

"How many must we be to be . . . a people?"

"Two or three are sufficient," Jesus replied.

Nothing else was said that night but in the time to come Jesus' friends often repeated these words to each other, troubled by them.

# 83

The next morning Shimon came running to meet them on the road.

"I have just returned from the village of Kerasa," he said to Jesus. "I went ahead because I have relatives there. When I told them I was with you, they pleaded with me to bring you to them."

"What do they want?"

"They have heard much about you from those who have traveled to the other villages. It is enough for them to speak with you."

"Who do they say that I am?"

"That you are a teacher of wisdom. Although some say you are Elijah returned, others that you are gathering an army to lead to Jerusalem."

"Who do you tell them I am?"

Shimon studied his hands for a moment. "They are waiting in a field outside Kerasa but are impatient for they have come without food and are hungry."

"Take loaves and fishes to them," Jesus said. "As you see, I am coming slowly."

Shimon ran off, taking several friends with him. When they had done what Jesus requested, they came back. "The people want still more. They complain we have not brought them enough."

"Bring them what they want."

Several hours later they came to him again and said, "We brought more food and when the people had eaten they stood and returned to their homes. No one remains in the field."

# 84

Passing through Kerasa they walked up into the hills west of Galilee. Some of those who had been with them returned to their homes. Others joined them.

With Jesus and the Samaritan, they were Thaddeus, Martha, Nicodemus, Levi, Nathanael and Bartholomew, Eustacia, the coppersmith and his daughter, Devorah, Zakkai and Havah, Yaakov, Joram, Shimon and Amri, and Didymos.

Because of the early spring rains they took shelter for several days in the caves looking over the Jordan Valley.

Late one night someone entered the cave where Jesus and the Samaritan were sleeping. He touched Jesus on the shoulder. Jesus sat up and saw that it was Judas.

"I have just come from Jerusalem," Judas said. "There is much to tell. Come outside. The coals are still hot. I'll make a fire."

Jesus folded himself into his cloak and sat next to Judas who was leaning forward blowing on the remaining embers and gently covering them with sticks. The air was still. Thunder could be heard at a distance.

"Yohanan is dead," Judas began. "He was arrested by the temple guard. When he was found guilty of a crime, they brought him before the people and tortured him for three days before he died."

"What was the crime?"

"It is not known. They also executed his followers. All that they could find. And many others as well who had never heard of Yohanan. It is said they are afraid of rebellion when the crowds come to the city for passover."

"Did you speak with Pilatus?"

"I had an audience with Pilatus. But he did not want to talk of these things. 'It is the concern of the priests,' he said. Then he said, 'Insurrectionists are common, true teachers rare. Tell me whether there be any. What else can you say about your Galilean rabbi?' I told him more about you. He asked me many questions. I repeated your stories. He wants to talk with you himself. 'Tell your teacher I would be honored,' he said."

Shimon, Martha, the Samaritan woman, and several others, awakened by their voices, came and sat with them. To the south of them lightning illumined the interior of the gathering clouds.

"Yohanan was not an insurrectionist," Jesus said. "It is not he who frightens the Romans."

"The people suffer and the Romans know that," Judas explained. "Rumors of rebellion are everywhere. Insurrectionists are said to be coming to Jerusalem in disguise. Many are expecting the arrival in the city of a 'messiah,' but of that I understand little."

"Yohanan thought the reign of satan would be ended by the hand of God," Jesus said. "He prophesied destruction but he would not himself touch the sword. The insurrectionists believe that they are the hand of God. For them there is nothing but the sword."

Judas knelt and placed a pot of cold gruel on the flames now freshened by a rising wind.

"There are to be more executions," he said. "The soldiers have erected crosses, hundreds of them, on a hill outside Jerusalem. There is said to be great danger for those who are there to celebrate your 'passover.'"

Jesus looked across the fire at the Samaritan. She said nothing, only nodded. He stood and walked into the dark. She followed.

"What is the meaning of these words of Judas?" he asked her.

Lightning was now touching the hills behind them. Thunder echoed across the lake.

"Judas doesn't understand," she said, "that he has become Pilatus's fool. Pilatus has made him the calf he wants you to follow. He wants to bring you . . . ," she paused for the thunder, ". . . to the knife of Rome."

After standing together for a while in silence, they returned to the others. The wind was blowing ribbons of sparks from the fire into the darkness.

"What will you do now?" Thaddeus asked Jesus.

Didymos sat next to him. "Will you go to Jerusalem?"

Jesus met Didymos's gaze. "I am going to Jerusalem," he said.

Then Judas spoke. "These are the words of Pilatus: 'If your teacher shares my desire for peace, I will share my table with him.' Do you have an answer for the governor?"

"Yes. I have an answer."

# 85

Shimon lay awake thinking of Judas's report that Jerusalem was expecting a messiah. He puzzled over Jesus' words for Pilatus: I have an answer. There can be no doubt, he said to himself, that Jesus is sent by God to begin the final struggle against Rome.

Certain that Jesus wanted to keep his great work in Jerusalem a secret, but knowing he would not say so directly, Shimon went to Jesus in the morning with a subtly worded question.

"Visionaries speak of the glorious kingdom that God will establish when the empire has been destroyed," he said. "Are we going to Jerusalem to join the building of this kingdom?"

"Be wary of visionaries. They can raise us to grand but false hopes."

"But you speak of bringing Rome to an end. Can there be a grander vision?"

"I ask you to do something far more difficult: Turn away from Rome. Else everything you do is the work of Rome."

"This is all? But what can come of an act the world will never notice?"

"This knowledge is withheld from you."

"Shall we then do nothing?"

"Act in faith."

"Faith?"

"Do what you must, but know you will be surprised."

When Jesus saw that Shimon was perplexed, he told this story:


A king, in grief over the loss of his queen, decided he would honor her by building a grand city in her name. He summoned the royal architects and builders and announced his plan.

Opening a map of the realm, he pointed to a high hill rising over a valley. "Build it here," he said, "where it will have a commanding view of the surrounding country."

The architects began their drawings at once and the builders sent word through the land, calling all available laborers and craftsmen to assemble at the foot of the summit and prepare for the great task ahead.

"No one is to live in the city," the king declared, "until the work is finished and it has been properly consecrated."

The laborers and craftsmen hastily built shelters for themselves just across the river from the site of the new city. When the final plans were published, the king's subjects were astonished. Never had they seen such ambitious and ingenious designs. Construction was begun immediately.

The workers, since they could see years of labor ahead, gradually brought their families to their expanding settlement. Their careless shelters were rebuilt. Merchants appeared. Soldiers were required to keep order in the teeming community.

Because of his age, the king ordered an accelerated pace of construction. More workers were brought in.

When taxes were raised, there were uprisings of subjects unhappy with the burdens of the project. These were quickly dealt with. Shortly after that, however, there were others. The king was forced to reach deeply into his treasury to keep peace in the realm. Building slowed, causing distress among the population of workers. As it slowed still more, they struggled to find ways of living with diminished wages.

The king's death made little difference to the workers and their families. A few still made their way up to the site each day but they were scarcely able to stay ahead of the rot and decay in what had already been done.

Years passed, then generations. Now no one bothers to cross the river and make the long climb to the summit except an occasional wanderer who stands in the vanishing ruins to look down at the great city on the other side of the valley.

# 86

Jesus woke them before sunrise the next morning. Passover was only days away. Because Nathanael's condition had worsened and Havah could no longer support him alone, they would have to walk slowly.

They came down a long hill to a ford over the Jordan River. When they had crossed, they met a small group standing in the road, as though expecting them. They were three men and two women with a much older woman partly supported by one of the men.

The old woman suddenly darted from the group and stepped with a pained limp toward Jesus and his friends.

Jesus stopped and waited for her to approach. The Samaritan looked from the old woman's face to Jesus' and back again. "This is your mother. And your brothers and sisters." Jesus nodded.

Miryam, her body bent, looked up at Jesus with a fierce and unblinking eye. Already small in stature, she now seemed even slighter.

"Your father is dead."

She waited but Jesus said nothing.

"We have heard about you, pretending to be a rabbi and a wonderworker."

She looked sharply at the Samaritan woman, then at his friends.

"I see it is true what they say of you. You dress in the rags of a beggar. Shoeless. Living in the open with no more shelter than a sparrow. Followed by these . . . You are a scandal for us."

She turned and looked at his brothers and sisters. They had not moved or spoken.

"Your brothers are doing your father's work and have families. You belong in your father's place."

"My father's place will remain empty," Jesus said to her.

"You are his firstborn and therefore bound."

"It was necessary to be bound to my father when I was a child, yes, but I did not learn to be his servant. Without intending it, he taught me instead to live free of all servitude."

"In a dream I saw the meaning of this 'freedom,'" Miryam said. She told Jesus this dream:

A young hawk, long before its time, announced with a great cry that it was ready to take its first flight. It did so and was met at once by terrible dangers. Young as it was, however, it had just enough skill and daring to escape these dangers.

But the bird was also foolish. One day it saw a great serpent and longed to feed on it. It seized the serpent at once and carried it heavenward. But this time the young hawk had gone far beyond its powers. The serpent twisted out of its talons and devoured it.

"Just then I woke," Miryam added. "I knew the dream was an oracle and that I was being sent to find you."

"There is much the dream does not see," Jesus said. "I will not come back with you. Let the others take up my father's work."

Jesus knelt before her. He took her hand and pressed it to his lips then stood, looked deeply into the faces of his brothers and sisters, and stepped back into the road. His friends went with him as he continued toward Jerusalem.

His mother kept him in her gaze until he had passed out of sight, then walked slowly after him.

# 87

As they drew near the city of Jericho, Shimon questioned the decision to continue on to Jerusalem. "This is a time of great danger. Rumors of coming violence are everywhere in the city. The temple guard and the governor's soldiers are already in the streets and vigilant. Innocent people are being publicly executed as an exemplary warning."

"Why is this a reason not to go?" Jesus asked.

"Your mother's dream," said Amri, "should be warning enough."

"There is a truth in my mother's dream," he said to Amri, "but it is a sleeper's truth. Those awake know that when the serpent has devoured the hawk it will fall to its death."

"I know nothing of the serpent," Martha said. "But I know there are many who will listen to a voice of peace and healing. They are a field ripe for harvest."

"No, Martha," Jesus said quietly. "The time for us to reap has not come. This will be a harvest of iron and blood."

"The real meaning of the dream," Levi said, "is that unless the serpent and the hawk die together, the serpent is still loose upon the earth." No one listened to his words.

# 88

As they continued along the road bordering the river, they found themselves in a lengthening column of pilgrims making their way to Jerusalem for passover. Because there were many tales of the state of tension in the city, a spirit of anticipation and dread had taken hold.

"They make you stand over a pointed stake until your legs give out," one of the pilgrims said to any who would listen. Then making a picture of it with his hands, he added, "The stake runs you through like this and comes out here, sometimes here."

"They cut the skin off your face so you look like a skull with bulging eyes," said another, sucking in his lips in a mocking demonstration. "Then you beg for the soldiers to finish you off but they keep you alive."

Jesus ignored them and kept walking silently ahead.

# 89

That evening, when they paused for the night, they talked quietly with each other about what they had heard and what lay ahead.

"This is the time to look for signs of his power," Shimon confided to those most troubled by the stories they had heard.

"No," said the coppersmith. "To enter the city with Jesus just now is reckless. How could we not draw the attention of the soldiers?"

When the dark came, the coppersmith quietly left with his daughter, leading the aged Nicodemus by the hand. Others joined them.

Zakkai, sharing these fears, came to Jesus. "If you turned away now and went to the desert, even to the mountains beyond," he said, "many would follow. We would live by your teachings and be a people together."

"How would this free us from Rome?" Jesus replied. "If we are in flight, we are in flight from Rome. If we are safe, we are safe from Rome. Rome would be closer to us than the food we eat and the words we speak. We cannot be a people in Rome without confronting Rome."

Others, hearing what Jesus was discussing with Zakkai, sat down with them.

"But you taught us to be oblivious to Rome, to let it die in our hearts," Joram said. "How are we to confront Rome if it has died in our hearts?"

"If it has died," Jesus said to him, "then Rome must see its death in us."

"What is there to see?"

"They will see the mortality in all that they do, that their boundaries are without force. They will see that no absolutes remain."

"For us," Devorah declared, "God alone is absolute."

"If so," Jesus said, "then God too must come to an end."

"Deny God?" she asked, astonished.

"God is not to be denied," Jesus answered, "for God is either beyond our comprehension, sharing nothing with us, or among us, sharing everything."

Devorah looked at Jesus, astonished. "How then could God be God?"

"How else could we be human?"

For a long time no one spoke. Then Thaddeus asked, "If we go to Jerusalem with you, we go as a people, as you said. But how will they know us as a people?"

"It is not necessary that we be known. It matters only that we know them."

When they said nothing more, Jesus told this story:

A prosperous farmer had but one child, a son. When he was old enough, the young man asked his father for his inheritance.

"But you have here all you need," the father said.

"What I have here," the boy replied, "is what you have provided me. I am ready to make my own way in the world."

"Where would you go?"

"To the city."

"The ways of the city are very different from those of the country."

"I have been there many times with you."

"Your inheritance is not large."

"But the opportunities are many."

"The boy is a dreamer," the father thought to himself, "and untried by the world. But he is a greater treasure to me than all I own. Perhaps it is time for him to be tested."

Full of plans, the young man bid a warm farewell to his father and set off.

When years passed without word, the farmer came to believe his son was dead. He buried his grief in labor, greatly adding to his land and animals.

Once, while leading cattle to a distant market, he caught sight of a familiar figure working in the mire of a swinery.

The old man sent the cattle on with a servant, changed into the rags of a field worker, and took his place next to his son. In time the two fell into conversation. Not recognizing his father, the son told him how he had wasted his inheritance and now was ashamed to go home.

The old man said little but continued to work at his son's side, the two of them sharing their meager income. Not until his father died and the son had inherited his estate did he know the true identity of his aged friend. He divided the land and animals among his father's servants, taking the smallest part for himself.

Jesus' friends waited.

"Is this all there is to the story?"

"Should there be more?"

"Why didn't the old man reveal himself to his son?"

"He revealed himself fully. He saw there was no other way."

# 90

They rose before dawn and began the long climb to the city. The sun came over the mountain ahead of them into a cloudless sky. They held their hands over their eyes as they walked.

When the midday heat came, Jesus saw that the Samaritan was weak. Though there was no shade they sat at the side of the road. He held a corner of his cloak above her.

Shimon and Amri, knowing the day would be long, had been careful to bring loaves and a flask with them.

They passed the wine to Jesus. Jesus lifted it to the lips of the Samaritan but took none himself; so too with the loaf. When she had eaten, he passed the bread and the cup to the others.

They slept and when the day was cooler they stood to continue their journey.

As he lifted the Samaritan to her feet, Jesus saw that she had a fever. "You can go no further," he said to her.

Just then a herder passed, leading a heifer he hoped to sell to the priests for sacrifice. When he saw that the Samaritan was ill, he nodded to her to climb onto the animal. He then threw his cloak over her shoulders. Jesus walked behind them.

# 91

As they came close to the city, there was a heightened urgency in the stream of pilgrims. Voices grew louder.

Hawkers were everywhere, selling dried fruit and citron gruel, head shawls, palm and olive branches. The prominent and the wealthy, led by slaves clad in royal costume, barked severe threats to those in their way. Beggars, most of them children, many of them deformed, cried out for attention or exposed their ghastly stumps. Now and then bold voices announced their enmity for Roman rule and the priests corrupted by it. Others, risking their lives, even prophesied the rise of a new king or the coming of God's inexhaustible wrath.

But the greater part of the crowd ignored these clamorers. Driven forward by their piety, they stared with amazement at the great walls and the buildings rising above them.

As the throng pushed through the narrowed opening to the city, all voices went still. A dark awareness came over the people when they saw the greatness of their number, for they knew the danger of it. So did the Roman guard. Never out of sight, standing in small groups, their weapons conspicuous, the soldiers studied the faces around them for furtive glances or gleams of madness, for they knew how easily this river of pilgrims could become a flood of rage and violence.

The crowd gave way as several officers of the palace guard led into their midst a group of prisoners just released by the governor as a gesture of good will.

The prisoners, blinded by their captors, confused by the hushed gasping of the crowd, held tightly to each other. Their skin was pale from years in unlighted cells. The odor of animal cages came from them.

The people stepped back, avoiding contact.

Jesus approached a young man shuffling on the bent sticks he used for crutches. "What was your crime?"

The cripple, suspicious, asked, "Who are you?"

"A friend," Jesus said. He held the young man's hands to his face.

When the man had studied the features of Jesus' face with his fingertips, he said, "I laughed at a drunken soldier clowning for his companions. He took me to prison and did this." He turned to show where the tendons behind his knees had been severed.

# 92

Jesus felt a strong hand on his arm. He looked up at a shrouded figure, saw that it was Judas, but did not speak his name.

"Pilatus sent me to find you," he said in a lowered voice. "I am to lead you to the palace. But I bribed the guards and learned that they were ordered to arrest you." He paused. "I have come in disguise to warn you. Pilatus will surely execute you. Why, I don't know. But I know you must flee at once."

Jesus looked at the Samaritan. She had fallen asleep on the neck of the heifer. The herder stood beside her, his impatience showing. When Jesus understood that the man needed to sell the animal, he gathered the woman in his arms and put her where she could sit against the stall of a water seller.

Judas came close and said, "Time is short. I must go before the guards recognize me and seize you."

"Go quickly, then, and take the others with you," Jesus answered.

"Where should I take them?"

"Leave the city and spend the night wherever you can."

Judas walked into the crowd and the others followed. They were Amri and his brother Shimon; the young scribe Joram; Martha; Levi; Nathanael and Havah; the widow Devorah; Didymos; Zakkai and Bartholomew; Thaddeus; and Yaakov.

# 93

When they were gone, Jesus begged a small supply of water from the water seller. He knelt and held it for the Samaritan. "Drink all of it," he said.

When she finished she looked at him and asked, "Are you afraid?"

"Yes," he said. "And you?"

Before she could answer, someone placed a foot on Jesus' hand. He saw that it was the thick sandal of a soldier. The feet of soldiers were all around them.

# 94

They brought Jesus before Pilatus.

"Unbind him."

The guards backed into the shadows.

"Stand there, where I can see you."

The governor slowly circled him, examining the marks of dried blood showing the treatment of his jailers. He shook his head and looked darkly at the guards but said nothing.

Swallows passed in and out of the great windows.

"You are Jesus, the teacher."

"My name is Jesus."

"I did not think you so young. You speak Greek."

"I am a Galilean."

"It is said you Jews expect the arrival of a 'messiah.' Some think you are this 'messiah.' Do you make this claim of yourself?"

"No."

"Do you say then that you are not?"

"Am I armed?" Jesus said. "Have you seen my . . . army?"

"Others believe you are a king in disguise."

"How could this blood be a disguise?"

"Are you, as they say, sent of God?"

"If I am sent of God, so are you. So are these," Jesus said, indicating the guards.

"You say this," Pilatus replied, "after you have been in their hands for two days? What kind of a God would send such brutes?"

"Any God who sends one person to correct another will eventually require torture."

"My judges think you are dangerous to the empire."

"Any empire I threaten no soldier can defend."

"Are you falsely charged? Speak up so I can hear you above the sounds of the street."

"I am not innocent."

"You are a strange prisoner. My cells are filled with men and women who never tire of declaring their innocence. To what then do you confess?"

"Neither am I guilty. This is not a matter of law."

"Bring a bench for this prisoner," Pilatus commanded the guards. "I don't want him to collapse before I finish with him. You are all dismissed. I will continue privately."

The governor called for a servant. A tray of food was set before him.

"I would share this with you but it would be a cruelty. You would live much longer into the execution. Better for you that you die quickly."

He lifted a cup and stared at the prisoner. The swallows' scratchy fussing could be heard above the governor's throne.

"Yes, I have decided to execute you. This interrogation has another use. You said it is not an issue of law. More. Say more about that. How is it then that you are not innocent?"

"No one is innocent who lives in a society cruel and unjust as this."

"How else shall we judge innocence if not by law?" Pilatus answered.

"What laws have I broken that you arrested me?"

"You are a threat to the order of the empire."

"The only danger I am to you is that I see what you see."

Pilatus stared at his prisoner but said nothing.

"You see that the laws of the empire are empty," Jesus said.

"Because they answer not to justice but to power, you know they are not laws at all."

"You are hastening your execution with these careless words."

"I have no need of this interrogation. You do."

Pilatus broke off a piece of bread, held it for a moment, then put it back.

"I see that your friend Judas is correct. I paid him to instruct me in the teachings of the Judean sages. You alone he praised. But your Judas is also a fool. He does not know what I know— and what you know—that the teaching of peace is more dangerous than open rebellion. Those who take up arms against Rome can only strengthen Rome."

Jesus waited.

"But I am no fool," Pilatus continued. "Better that you be remembered as a martyred leader than as a teacher of peace. The rage of your followers will make the use of force essential to civil order. My soldiers will be praised as keepers of the peace."

"You are too late," Jesus said. "What you call my 'teaching' has gone before you. The words are as free to pass in and out of your empire as these swallows."

"You are clever in your speech. Judas saw it well. He is an excellent student. But still he does not understand. Certainly the poor will speak against poverty. What else can we expect of them? But when someone indifferent to poverty speaks against it, the social order is severely threatened. And when someone indifferent to power . . . "

Pilatus sighed and pointed at the ceiling.

"These swallows. Each year the slaves sweep their nests away. The next year they are back, with their noise and filth. But how can I bar the windows against them without making this room a cage?"

"To be Rome to the world is to be Rome to yourself."

Pilatus looked cunningly at Jesus. "This is why you are dangerous to Rome. We are at war with these birds but they're not at war with us—so we can't defeat them."

"You killed Yohanan. Were you at war with him?"

"Just so much feathers and dung. We brushed it away."

"And the insurrectionists? Do they threaten you?"

"Threaten Rome? These are the rodents on which the imperial eagle fattens itself."

Pilatus went to the window and looked down at the street.

"If the genius of ruling has not left us, we will not oppose your words. There is a far better way to remove their danger, though their danger is great. We will make them our own. When Rome speaks on behalf of the poor, Rome will be seen as the enemy of great evils. We cannot do away with these loathsome birds so we declare them royal swallows. We will do the same with your words, or with some of your words—declare them an imperial testament."

Seating himself, he opened his hands to the prisoner.

"It is so, you are not a criminal. You will be executed with thieves and murderers but without explanation. Your followers will know you were unjustly punished. The better for us. For this reason I have ordered most of them released. Yes, we arrested them also. We found them in a garden outside the city gate. But they are now free. Except for the girl and the idiot. I gave those two to the soldiers."

He called for the guards and ordered them to take the prisoner away.

Pilatus sat where he was, unmoving, until the light was gone and the swallows were quiet. The food remained untouched.

# 95

The fever did not leave her until the evening of the second day after her release from prison.

Still weak, she walked slowly up toward the hill where the condemned had been executed. The public lanterns in the city had been extinguished. There was now no light but that of the stars. The hill raised its barbed crown against a cloudless sky.

There was no wind and, except for a faint cry of the slowly dying, the silence was complete.

She found Miryam coiled against the bottom of a cross like someone unborn, motionless as the dead. She leaned over her and saw that her eyes were open and lighted as with a vision.

"He is not dead," Miryam said.

The Samaritan touched the flesh of his leg, now swollen. The smell of carrion was about him.

"Come," she said to Miryam.

"I hear him singing."

The Samaritan studied his face in the starlight. His open mouth, black with flies, sounded with the hum of their feast.

"Come," she said again.

When she saw that Miryam would not leave, she sat with her to watch through the night. Not until dawn did she notice the raven, motionless, holding her in its gaze, close enough that she could see the dot of light in its eye.